Planning and Evaluating Human Services Programs

A RESOURCE GUIDE FOR PRACTITIONERS

Dr. Charles A. Maher
Professor Emeritus

Graduate School of Applied and Professional Psychology
Rutgers University

authorHOUSE®

AuthorHouse™
1663 Liberty Drive
Bloomington, IN 47403
www.authorhouse.com
Phone: 1-800-839-8640

The book provides educational information about how to design, implement, and evaluate programs in human services settings. This information presented in this book is intended to educate the reader to principles and procedures of program planning and evaluation. The use of this material, however, should not be considered as being prescriptive in nature. The material will not guarantee that any program which is designed and implemented using these principles and procedures will be effective or otherwise considered as having value. Decisions about program design, implementation, and evaluation should be made by the individuals who are involved in the planning and evaluation process, within the relevant context.

Published by AuthorHouse 4/30/2012

ISBN: 978-1-4685-6135-7 (sc)
ISBN: 978-1-4685-6133-3 (e)

Library of Congress Control Number: 2012904706

This book is printed on acid-free paper.

table of contents

preface

The information contained in this book has been developed and refined by me over a period of 35 years. This information is based on my research, teaching, and professional practice as a core faculty member of the Graduate School of Applied and Professional Psychology at Rutgers University and as a licensed psychologist.

During this period of time, I taught the course, "Planning and Evaluating Human Services Programs", which I created, to about 700 students. Most of these students have been doctoral students in clinical, school, and organizational psychology while others have come from such areas as counseling, social work, public policy, and nursing. The information which is contained in this book was the curriculum for that course. It is just as relevant today as it was years ago as a resource for individuals who are involved in professional practice and in a range of disciplines.

This book, *Planning and Evaluating Human Services Programs: A Resource Guide for Practitioners*, consists of a framework, a set of principles, and a range of procedures that can be used to guide the practitioner toward successful completion of four program planning and evaluation phases. These phases involve:

1. **Clarification Phase**: Identifying a target population of people who may benefit from a human services program; determining particular needs of the target population so that a program may be designed; and assessing the relevant context in which those needs are embedded.

2. **Design Phase**: Based on specific needs of the target population that have been identified and, within the relevant context, formulating a program that has a clear purpose and goals and that is linked to practical methods, procedures, and activities.

3. **Implementation Phase**: Facilitating the implementation of the program; monitoring how the program is being implemented; and making adjustments in the program's design, as may be indicated.

4. **Evaluation Phase**: Making informed judgments about the extent to which the goals of the program have been attained; understanding the reactions of program participants to the program and related factors; and using the resulting evaluative information for program improvement.

Throughout the years, I have been told by many former students and colleagues that the material in the book has been invaluable to them as they assist their clients with program planning and evaluation activities.

Moreover, I have had many requests for the information which is contained in this book from human services practitioners throughout the world. Heretofore, I had provided this material only to my students as an unpublished document. Now, I believe that the time is right to provide the information to other practitioners.

I hope this book has value for your professional practice.

Charles A. Maher, PsyD
Professor Emeritus
Graduate School of Applied and Professional Psychology
Rutgers University
February 2012

acknowledgements

I want to thank the many doctoral students who completed my course, Planning and Evaluating Human Services Programs, and who successfully defended dissertations in this area, over the years, at the Graduate School of Applied and Professional Psychology, Rutgers University. Your enthusiasm for program planning and evaluation as well as your energy in being involved in projects that had to do with program design, implementation, and evaluation are very much appreciated. I have learned a lot from you in the process. Furthermore, I am pleased to have had numerous opportunities to have used the principles and procedures which are contained in this book in collaboration with many program directors, administrators, and executives in a range of human services agencies, institutions, and organizations, worldwide, during the past 35 years. This consultation work has been very gratifying to me and it has helped to shape my approach to enhancement of performance at individual, group, and organizational levels. Moreover, I am indebted to Donald Peterson, my former dean at the Graduate School of Applied and Professional Psychology, for encouraging me to create, document, teach, and apply the principles and procedures that are contained in this book and to bring this material into the real world. Finally, I want to thank Jennifer Gibson for unswerving support in the preparation of the manuscript for the book.

chapter one

૭

OVERVIEW OF THE RESOURCE GUIDE

Human services programs exist in many forms and operate in diverse organizations in areas of business, industry, education, government, health care, and other sectors of society. This has been the case for many years; it is a reality at present and, no doubt will be so for years to come. Moreover, human services programs are targeted to a wide range of psychological and educational needs of people from infant, early childhood, adolescent, to adult age groups.

While human service programs are different and diverse in terms of people served, important needs of these populations, and relevant contextual factors, a common core of principles and procedures can be applied across program types, situations, and settings. These principles and procedures can be applied by an individual practitioner, a work group, a multi-disciplinary team, or other configurations of professionals to increase the likelihood that valuable programs will be provided to human beings in need. Most fundamentally, though, these principles and procedures, which are covered thoroughly in this book, are part of the *process* of the program planning and evaluation, an important, albeit often overlooked, entity of professional practice—no matter what the disciplinary base of the practitioner.

The process of program planning and evaluation is, in essence, what this book is all about. The process is reflected by the gathering, analyzing, interpreting, and using of information so that evaluative judgments can be made about the worth or merit of a program (i.e., for program evaluation purposes). Relatedly, program relevant information can be used for deciding how to place a program in operation so that goals can be attained and needs met (i.e., for program planning purposes). With precise understanding of the process of program planning and evaluation, coupled with skill at application of its principles and procedures, the likelihood is increased that valuable programs will result for people in need.

This book is not a 'cookbook', nor a quick-fix document. Rather, it is a description of the program planning and evaluation process that I have developed over the years, along with the principles and procedures which structure the process. More specifically, the book literally provides guidelines for how to proceed to accomplish four separate, yet interrelated, program planning and evaluation tasks. These are:

1. *Clarification* of meaningful conditions having to do with program need, context, and the target population to be served.

2. *Design* of a program, based on the clarification information.

3. *Implementation* of the program according to its design, with necessary changes made, based on accurate information.

4. *Evaluation* of the worth or merit of the program as a basis for continuous improvement.

As a result of a thorough understanding of the material contained in this book, you will be able to do the following as a human services practitioner: (a) personally influence the process of program planning and evaluation; (b) recognize variations in the process that have controllable causes so that you can make necessary adjustments; (c) decide what principles and procedures to apply and when to do so; and (d) specify particular methods, techniques, and instrument that can be developed or selected to accomplish the above-mentioned tasks of program planning and evaluation. Your use of the information in this book will not be a straight-forward, linear event. Rather, it is likely to result in some personal frustration, conceptual ambiguity, mastering programmatic thinking, continuous personal improvement, satisfaction from learning a valuable technology for helping others to work toward worthwhile human services programs, and enjoyment.

Best wishes on the journey.

chapter two

PARAMETERS OF PROGRAM PLANNING AND EVALUATION

Table 2.1 is a visual portrayal of the Systems Framework for Program Planning and Evaluation. With a sound, thorough understanding of the framework and its consistent concepts, the likelihood is increased that you will facilitate the provision of valuable programs and services to target populations of people in need and to your professional clients who serve those people.

The Systems Framework for Program Planning and Evaluation (Table 2.1) rests on the notion of a program as seen in its broadest sense, as a configuration of resources—human, technological, informational, financial, temporal, and physical—organized to add value to an individual, group, or organization. In this regard, value-added programs are provided through control and influence of the process of program planning and evaluation, which involves the application of its principles and procedures.

Constituent Concepts of the Systems Framework

The Systems Framework for Program Planning and Evaluation (Table 2.1 matrix) consists of three constituent concepts. These are:

1. **Program Level**—this is the vertical dimension of the matrix, where three such levels have been delineated (Organizational, Group, Individual).

2. **Planning and Evaluation Process**—this is the horizontal dimension of the matrix, where four phases of the process have been identified (Clarification, Design, Implementation, Evaluation).

3. **Planning and Evaluation Technology**—this is represented as the intersection of the vertical dimension and horizontal dimension of the matrix that forms 12 cells. Within each cell, depending on the program level and type, particular methods, instruments and procedures are used.

Each constituent concept is discussed further below.

Table 2.1: Systems Framework for Program Planning and Evaluation

"LEVELS"	"PHASE"			
	Clarification	Design	Implementation	Evaluation
Organizational	1	2	3	4
Group	5	6	7	8
Individual	9	10	11	12

Program Level

A program is a configuration of resources, organized to add value to an individual, group, or organization. The kinds of resources that are organized are the same for any level of program, although the quantity (volume) of resources will differ by level. The resources for any individual, group, or organizational program will include some combination of the following:

- **Human Resources**—people who are involved in the program as participants; program implementers; administrators; supervisors; consultants; other stakeholders.

- **Technological**—methods used by implementers and participants to facilitate goal attainment; materials such as books, worksheets, and software; equipment; activities; manuals; procedures, etc.

- **Informational Resources**—information to guide and direct a program's human resources including policies, philosophy, mission statement, goals, goal indicators, etc.

- **Financial Resources**—currencies (e.g., dollars) that are considered necessary to support program design and implementation including funds procured through local stakeholders, external public agencies, and private sources.

- **Temporal Resources**—amount of time that is available, or that might reasonably be made available, for the program to be designed and implemented.

- **Physical Resources**—facilities wherein the program can be implemented.

A human services program can be said to be worthwhile, or meritorious, when it can be documented, in a technically justifiable way (reliable, valid), that *value has been added* to the target population, following program implementation. In this regard, program value has to do with two separate, albeit interrelated conditions: (a) positive growth and development of the target population in such domains as cognitive development, affective functioning, and psychomotor proficiency; and (b) associated positive change in target population accomplishments (e.g., enhanced productive quality; effective instruction; societal contribution).

As seen in Table 2.1, programs exist at various levels. In this regard, it has been found useful at the level of professional practice to delineate programs at three particular levels, as follows:

- **Organizational Program Level**—programs at this level typically encompass all members of an organization (e.g., all company employees; all high school students; all government workers). As such, these programs are broad in scope and typically focus on dissemination of information and not skills training.

- **Group Program Level**—programs at this level focus on a well-defined group of people (target population) with a particular set of needs, but not all organizational members. As such, these programs are likely to be customized with emphasis on skills training in addition to information dissemination.

- **Individual Program Level**—programs at this level are designed for one person, and as such, are not totally similar to any program provided to any other person.

For all programs at all levels to be provided to a target population, however, the program can benefit from a sound program *design*, that is based on a well understood and *clarified* situation, that is *implemented* according to design, and that is *evaluated* routinely and in a technically defensible manner. This state of affairs can happen through personal control of the process of program planning and evaluation, the second constituent concept of the Systems Framework (Table 2.1).

Planning and Evaluation Process

Table 2.1 delineates the four phases and important constituent activities of the process of planning and evaluation of a program, seen as the horizontal dimension of the matrix. In this regard, *planning* means the using of evaluation information for program improvement. Relatedly, *evaluating* denotes gathering, analyzing, and interpreting evaluation information, as a basis for program planning. Furthermore, *revising* refers to purposeful and routine activity that occurs throughout the planning and evaluation process.

The four phases of the process of program planning and evaluation are separate, yet they interrelate, in that these phases depend on one another, for successful application and control. More specifically, each phase also represents a process, in and of itself, that can be controlled and that includes activities that likewise are interrelated and dependent on one another. As such, the overall planning and evaluation process, and its phases and activities, can be termed as interactive and reflexive. Moreover, the process of program planning and

5

evaluation can be controlled by one person such as a professional services provider acting directly and independently, or the process can be controlled in a collaborative way such as by a work group or team.

The phases and activities of the process are:

1. 0 CLARIFICATION PHASE
    1.1 Specify the target population
    1.2 Determine needs of the target population
    1.3 Delineate the relevant context

2.0 DESIGN PHASE
    2.1 Describe program purpose and goals
    2.2 Consider program design alternatives
    2.3 Develop the program
    2.4 Document the program design

3.0 IMPLEMENTATION PHASE
    3.1 Review the program design
    3.2 Facilitate program implementation
    3.3 Monitor program process

4.0 EVALUATION PHASE
    4.1 Obtain program reactions
    4.2 Measure learning associated with the program
    4.3 Identify applications resulting from the program
    4.4 Judge program benefits and value

Each phase and its activities will be discussed thoroughly in subsequent sections of this book.

Planning and Evaluation Technology

The 12 cells of the matrix of the Systems Framework (Table 2.1) represent this third constituent concept. In this regard, planning and evaluation technology is the overarching term used to encompass particular methods, procedures, and instruments for program planning and evaluation. This technology is used for all activities of all phases of the process. However, although the process is the same at all program levels, the methods, procedures, and instruments will be different.

Thus, with respect to *Clarification* technology, particular methods, procedures, and instruments will be used for the activities of that phase (Table 2.1 matrix cells 1, 5, 9); *Design* technology with matrix cells 2, 6, 10; *Implementation* technology with matrix cells 3, 7, 11; *Evaluation* technology with matrix cells 4, 8, 12. Methods, procedures, and instruments that comprise the technology of each phase of the process will be considered in all of the subsequent chapters of the book.

chapter three

CLARIFICATION PHASE

In this chapter, the Clarification Phase is described in terms of its overarching purpose, constituent activities, technologies, and resulting products.

Purpose of the Clarification Phase

Without a clear understanding of a present situation that is of concern to a human services client and relevant to stakeholders, it is difficult, indeed impossible, to plan a program that adds value to an individual, group, or organization. Lack of clarity about a presenting situation – particularly about a target population, its needs, and relevant context within which those needs are embedded – fosters limited perspectives on how to add value in a programmatic way. Further, lack of clarity does not assure a controlled, predictable program planning and evaluation process. Alternatively, a well understood and *clarified* situation, especially when validated empirically, helps foster focused perspectives on how to add value and contributes to the program planning and evaluation process.

The Clarification Phase is the first of four major phases of the program planning and evaluation process. The purpose of this phase is to clarify the current situation that is of concern to the client and perhaps other stakeholders. This purpose is realized through a series of sequential, interrelated activities by which a program planning and evaluation consultant, or consultant team, gathers, analyzes, and interprets information. This resulting information allows sound (reliable, valid) understanding and agreement about a target population to be served, the needs of the target population that may be addressed by means of a program, and the relevant context within which those needs are embedded. As a result of appropriate use of these activities and technologies that pertain to these activities, a Clarification Report can be generated by the consultant for use by the client and others. As will be discussed subsequently, a Clarification Report is a conceptual and empirical base for making decisions having to do with how to design a program (Design Phase).

Overview of the Activities of the Clarification Phase

Based on the above purpose, there are three major activities of the Clarification Phase. These activities are described as follows:

1.1 **Specify the target population** that may be a candidate for a well-designed human service program.

1.2 **Determine needs of the target population** that may be addressed by a human service program in that the needs are psychological and educational in nature and scope.

1.3 **Delineate the relevant context**, wherein needs of the target population are embedded, in order to enhance understanding of the readiness of the target population and the organization for a human service program.

The above three activities are sequential in that one must follow the other for a well understood and *clarified* situation to be documented. Further, these activities are interrelated in that the information generated from one activity serves to guide how to proceed with the next activity including the technologies (e.g., methods, techniques, instruments, procedures) to be used as part of the activity. Finally, the activities are reflexive in that changes in one activity and the resulting information may require re-routing to a previously completed activity.

In the next section of this chapter, the first activity of the Clarification Phase – Specify the Target Population – is discussed.

1.1 Specify the Target Population

Through this program planning and evaluation activity, a target population is specified that can be considered as a candidate for a human service program. In this regard, a target population is the individual (i.e., "n of 1" or population of 1), group, or organization (all people therein) for whom a program can be designed and implemented – if valid need exists and if the relevant context indicates readiness.

It is very important to specify the target population, for various reasons. These reasons include

- The number of people who may be in need of a program can be documented, thereby informing the client, others, and yourself as consultant about the possible scope of a program.

- Comparisons can be made about the target population's parameters (e.g., age, psychoeducational characteristics) in relation to relevant eligibility criteria for a program.

- Comparisons can be made between and among the target population with non-target populations, as a basis for deciding whether reasonable and appropriate comparisons can be made for program evaluation purposes.

- When there is concern about eventual dissemination of a program to other populations and similarities and differences need to be considered in making the dissemination decision.

- In order to decide how to plan for an assessment of target population needs.

- Other reasons.

In order to specify the target population that is of concern to the client and others, several tasks need to be accomplished by yourself with the client. These tasks are:

1.11 Determine the size (number) of the target population, exactly or in a reliable approximate way.

1.12 Describe relevant characteristics of the target population.

1.13 Given the size of the target population, decide whether and to what extent it needs to be segmented.

1.14 Document the target population in a clear and understandable manner.

Each of these tasks will be discussed below.

1.11 Determine the size of the target population

There are three methods that can be used to determine the size of the target population for program planning and evaluation purposes. These methods are:

- Interview
- Permanent Product Review
- Questionnaire

Interview. The interview method may be the most direct and economical approach, especially when the target population is clearly identifiable such as a "population of 1", or some other clearly identified quantity. In using the interview method, you essentially want an answer to the following question as it might be directed to a client or client designee:

- In order to determine the needs of the target population that are of concern, how many people comprise it?

Sometimes in using the interview method, it may not be clear as to what people comprise the target population. If so, it is recommended that, as an initial step, you include the larger number of specific groups or segments in the population (e.g., ED members and LD members as part of the larger population of at risk special education students; supervisors and managers as part of the larger population of organization leadership personnel). Subsequently, based on interview discussion and/or other information, it may be appropriate to segment the larger population and/or eliminate groups or segments altogether.

Permanent Product Review. The permanent product review method for determining the size of the target population for a human services program can best be used in a practical and economical way under several conditions. These conditions are:

- When there is likely to be a large number of people included in the population and it is not apparent as to the exact number and when the client or designee does not know the number.

- When the data are included as part of one or more electronic databases that are routinely updated.

- Other pertinent conditions.

In reviewing permanent product data, whether through manual files or a computerized database, consideration needs to be given by you to the reliability of the data. In this regard, an informed judgment must be made about whether the data are accurate not only with respect to quantity but also in terms of its timeliness. Toward making this kind of judgment, you often will need to rely on client self-report. Thus, you can query the client, in a straightforward yet tactful way, about the quantity, accuracy, and timeliness of the permanent product data that has been reviewed or that will be reviewed.

Questionnaire. The questionnaire method is best used to determine the size of the target population when (a) it is not clear how many people may be part of the target population and (b) target population members may be present over diverse geographical areas or organizational sites.

In using the questionnaire method, the instrument that you develop or select should possess the following qualities:

- A cover letter to the instrument, or a clear introduction to it, should be included. This document is intended to inform the respondent about the purpose or rationale for use of the questionnaire (e.g., to identify people who may have need for a new program).

- A clear, functional description or definition of the target population.

- Specific questions or items that, when responded to, will provide you with data about:

  o Quantity of people who fit the target population description.

  o Whether this number is an exact count or an estimate.

  o If the number is an estimate, the opinion of the respondent about the accuracy of the estimate (e.g., 80% accurate).

- A data or time frame within which you would like to receive the requested data.

- A means to contact you, and when to do so, if they have questions about your request.

- An expression of your appreciation for their compliance with your request (e.g., tangible product, report, relevant social expression).

- A guarantee of anonymity and confidentiality of response.

- Other qualities.

In some instances, this kind of questionnaire can be incorporated as part of a needs assessment instrument. However, on many occasions, such inclusion is not recommended because the request for census/quantity data on a target population may distract the person from completing the needs assessment aspect of the request, thereby confusing the different activities.

Naturally, it also is important that you seek to send the questionnaire to the people whom you believe have most accurate data knowledge and authorization to send it to you.

1.12 Describe relevant target population characteristics

This task is important in that it allows you and the client to get a more thorough understanding of the target population. Successful implementation of this task is important, though, only to the extent that the additional information obtained about the target population will help in making decisions about needs determination, context description, or program design matters. Before obtaining additional information about target population characteristics, you should have a programmatic rationale for obtaining such information.

The task of describing relevant target characteristics can be successfully implemented through one of the three methods already discussed for the task of determining target population size (see Task 1.11 above). Hence, the parameters of these methods will not be discussed here. Again, these methods are:

- Interview
- Permanent Product Review
- Questionnaire

The way that you proceed in using these methods for the current task is the same as the previous one. In fact, both tasks typically follow one another as part of the same interview, permanent product review, or as part of the same questionnaire instrument. In this regard, however, the key question or issue that you need to consider with respect to the client is the following:

- What target population characteristics, if known, may guide subsequent program planning and evaluation activities?

In order to help you and the client answer this question, it is useful to place characteristics

11

of any target population into possible program relevant characteristics categories. A program relevant characteristic category is one in which particular variables can be specified and on which data can be gathered, analyzed, and interpreted with respect to a target population. Here is an example set of characteristic categories which may be program relevant, in whole or in part, for a particular target population:

- Demographic Characteristics
  o Age
  o Gender
  o Experience at a job or task
  o Other

- Social-Community Characteristics
  o Cultural values/expectation
  o Linguistic patterns
  o Familial constellation
  o Other

- Education Characteristics
  o Level of academic achievement
  o Level of functional living skills
  o Vocational development
  o Other

- Psychological Characteristics
  o Social Skills
  o Personality traits/dispositions
  o Affective development
  o Other

- Physical Characteristics
  o Physical features
  o Motor development
  o Physical health
  o Other

The task of describing relevant target population characteristics also involves (a) gathering of the data (via interview, permanent product review, questionnaire); (b) analyzing the resulting data using appropriate statistical procedures, usually by means of descriptive statistics; (c) interpreting the meaning of the data; and (d) deciding how to use resulting information for subsequent program planning and evaluation.

1.13 Decide about segmentation of the target population

Segmentation of the target population involves dividing the larger group into meaningful, program relevant clusters, levels, divisions, or other stratifications. Segmentation of this type is usefully accomplished, based on descriptive information that already has been obtained about the size of the target population and its relevant characteristics.

Typically, a basic assumption is made when deciding to segment the target population. The assumption has to do with a belief that various segments of the target population possess characteristics that are distinct enough from one another that the needs of the segments (groups) may require different program designs or adaptions of some generic program design.

In deciding about segmentation of the target population, a key question that, if answered, can help facilitate the decision by you, the client, and other relevant stakeholders is the following one:

- What will knowing about particular segments of the target population mean for subsequent program planning and evaluation?

Naturally, if the answer is not clear, or you answer "nothing", then target population segmentation may not be useful or appropriate at the time. If target population segmentation seems to be appropriate, however, then the nature and scope of each segment then is delineated. Here are examples of factors or variables that may be program relevant segments:

- School
- Grade level
- Division
- Department
- Company (of a larger corporate entity)
- Disciplinary group (e.g., psychologists, executives)
- Diagnostic category
- Other

1.14 Documentation of the target population

The task of documentation of the target population, and relevant segments thereof, involves utilization of one or more of several methods. These methods involve description and display of data about number (quantity) and characteristics (quality) of the target population. These documentation methods include:

- Tabular display of target population data.
- Graphic display of such data (e.g., bar graphs, pie charts, line graphs).
- Narrative accounting of the data.
- Oral discussion of the data.

Documentation of program relevant information about size and characteristics of the target population is useful to the extent that it helps guide the second activity of the Clarification Phase of the program planning and evaluation process: Determine needs of the target population. This activity is discussed next.

1.2 Determine Needs of the Target Population

Once the target population has been specified, programmatic attention can focus on the activity of determining needs of the target population that may be addressed by means of a program. In this regard, a need is defined as a discrepancy between a current state of affairs having to do with psychological or educational functioning of the target population and a desired state of affairs pertinent to it. More specifically, a human service need can be said to exist when two situations prevail: (1) a *current state of affairs* that represents a psychological or educational state of the target which has been identified and that has been judged by the client, other stakeholders, and perhaps yourself, as being amenable to change or that is not satisfactory in some way; and (2) a *desired state of affairs* for the target population which has been delineated and that is considered as a positive advance over the current state. A need is not a solution, such as the need for a particular type of program. Rather, a human service need has to do with the psychological or educational state of the target population. More basically, a need has to do with a human performance domain (e.g., cognition, socialization, communication, physical movement).

The activity of determining needs of a target population reflects a process of gathering, analyzing and interpreting information about the target population and their needs and then making evaluative judgments about the nature, scope, and extent of needs. This process also is referred to as needs assessment and will be used synonymously with the term, needs determination, in the chapter. As with all program planning and evaluation activities and processes, however, there are several qualities of a sound approach. In this regard, four qualities of a sound needs assessment are:

1. **Practicality**—the needs assessment must be capable of being implemented in the organization or setting where the target population exists in a way that does not disrupt organizational routines (e.g., classroom instruction, a company's manufacturing process).

2. **Utility**—the needs assessment must allow for evaluative information to be procured that: (a) directs the client and other stakeholders in how to proceed with program planning; and/or (b) validates the nature, scope, and extent of needs of a target group in relevant psychological and educational domains.

3. **Propriety**—the needs assessment must adhere to all relevant rules, regulations, standards, and rights of the target population, relevant others in their lives, and organizational members. These strictures are both legal and ethical in nature.

4. **Technical Defensibility**—the needs assessment includes use of methods, procedures, and instruments that can be justified as being reliable as well as being valid for their intended purposes.

It is very important to conduct a sound needs assessment that encompasses the above qualities. Reasons to do so include the following:

- By identifying discrepancies between a current state of affairs and a desired state of affairs with respect to a target population, evaluative judgments can be made about the size of the discrepancy, or size of need. Relatedly, needs in various areas then can be prioritized, based on the estimated size of the discrepancy.

- A need (in the discrepancy sense) becomes a benchmark point of reference for context assessment and subsequent program design activities (e.g., goal setting that is based on needs).

- Without empirical documentation of need, the extent to which an evaluative judgment can be made about the worth of a program is limited. This is so because a program's worth (value) is determined in part in relation to each need it addresses. Thus, the more a program addresses and alleviates each need, the more valuable it is.

There are several steps that you can take with a client and stakeholders in determining needs of a target population. These steps apply to all program levels of the planning and evaluation process: individual, group, organizational. These steps are:

1.21 Identify psychological and educational domains on which needs assessment may focus.

1.22 Decide which domains are relevant for needs assessment.

1.23 For each relevant domain, delineate needs assessment questions that, when answered, will guide subsequent program planning.

1.24 Formulate a structure of needs that can guide needs assessment planning.

1.25 Specify variables on which data can be collected to answer each needs assessment question.

1.26 Develop and select methods, procedures, and instruments that will allow data to be collected as a basis for answering each needs assessment question.

1.27 Specify procedures for analysis and interpretation of the needs assessment results.

1.28 Delineate an approach for communication and use of needs assessment information.

1.29 Specify needs assessment roles, responsibilities, and timelines.

1.30 Place the needs assessment plan into an appropriate document.

1.31 Follow through on the needs assessment, using needs assessment protocols.

1.32 Construct a Needs Assessment Results Document.

Each of these aforementioned steps now will be discussed.

1.21 Identify psychological and education domains on which needs assessment may focus

At this point in the program planning and evaluation process, you have specified the target population with the client. In doing so, you no doubt have discussed with the client areas of psychological and educational concern with respect to the target population. Consequently, you probably have an idea about the focus of the needs assessment.

The intention of this initial step is to formulate a needs assessment strategy on relevant psychological and educational domains. In this regard, a domain is a set of behaviors or functions that can be grouped together and defined in relation to that group. For planning and evaluation of human services programs, these domains have to do with the psychology and education of the target population. In seeking to identify relevant psychological and educational domains on which needs assessment can focus, it is suggested that you ask and answer the following question for yourself, in collaboration with the client and other involved stakeholders:

- What are domains of the target population in which need seems to exist having to do with growth, development, and improvement of the target population?

In order to answer the above question, it is necessary to specify particular domains for needs assessment. Although these are no unitary set of agreed upon psychological and educational domains, here is a set of domains, and brief functional descriptions thereof, that has proven useful for needs assessment purposes at individual, group, and organizational program levels:

1. **Cognitive Domain**—this domain reflects functions of thinking, reasoning (analytic, synthetic), problem solving, as well as use of imagery for visual motor behavior rehearsal purposes.

2. **Affective Domain**—this domain reflects functions having to do with feelings, emotions, emotional control, and related affective dimensions (e.g., temperament).

3. **Socialization Domain**—this domain reflects functions of relating to individuals and groups in social contexts including social discourses and leadership dimensions.

4. **Communication Domain**—this domain reflects functions of speaking, listening, writing, and related communication dimensions.

5. **Educational Domain**—this domain reflects functions of academic achievement including arenas such as mathematics, language arts, reading, writing, science, social studies, etc.

6. **Vocational Domain**—this domain reflects functions having to do with performance in job and work situations, including job related technical skills.

7. **Psychomotor Domain**—this domain reflects functions involving fine motor development and gross motor movement including muscular coordination.

8. **Physical Domain**—this domain reflects functions having to do with senses of sight, sound, smell, taste, and touch along with cardiovascular and respiratory development.

In considering the above domains for needs assessment purposes, please note full well that they are not ranked in order nor should they be considered as being inclusive or exhaustive of all domain possibilities. The important task at this point is to decide with the client what domains are of concern.

1.22 Decide which domains are relevant for needs assessment

Once psychological and educational domains have been identified with the client, attention shifts to deciding which domains are the most relevant. In this regard, relevance is determined based on informed opinions of the client and other stakeholders about which needs can readily be addressed within their organization with respect to the target population. A judgment about this matter can be made by considering the organization's mission and purpose. Moreover, in conjunction with the client and others, you can ask and answer the following question:

- Given the psychological and educational domains that pertain to the target population, which domains are the most relevant for needs assessment, considering the purpose of the organization?

At this point, it is best to focus on making the above decision but not to consider yet whether one or more programs can be designed in response to needs in the relevant domains. A program is a solution, an intervention relative to a clearly described situation – target, need, context – that has yet to be determined. Hence, such specific program decision making is premature at this point in the program planning and evaluation process.

1.23 For each relevant domain, delineate needs assessment questions that, when answered, will guide subsequent program planning

Once the domains on which needs assessment will focus have been identified with respect to the target population, one or more needs assessment questions can be delineated for each domain. A needs assessment question is one that, when answered in a sound (reliable, valid) manner, will result in particular understandings for the client, other relevant stakeholders, and yourself with respect to the target population. These understandings are:

- The extent to which a discrepancy (need) exists between a current state of affairs and a desired state of affairs for a target population, in a relevant domain. This discrepancy (need) will be documented with empirical results (i.e., as an answer to the needs assessment question).

- Areas of need that warrant additional data collection and/or priority action for subsequent program planning activities (e.g., context assessment).

Delineation of one or more needs assessment questions for each relevant domain is important as part of an overall, planned needs assessment strategy for several reasons. These reasons are:

- A thoughtfully stated needs assessment question helps the client, stakeholders, and yourself pinpoint important areas of need or potential need of the target population. With such a focus on the needs assessment question, just how to measure and document need becomes more readily apparent than without a clearly stated needs assessment question.

- The task of answering a needs assessment question is a professionally familiar way of dealing with how to proceed, based on an answer to the question.

- Relatedly, a needs assessment report can be organized and developed around a series of needs assessment questions and answers.

- Other reasons.

A recommended method for delineating needs assessment questions for each relevant domain of the target population is the following method, used in conjunction with the client and others:

1. Specify the relevant domain on which needs assessment will focus (e.g., communication domain for LD students)

2. Segment the domain to a more functional entity when considered as being desirable (e.g., oral communication for LD students)

3. For the segmented domain, list one or more questions that may be appropriate needs assessment questions (e.g., To what extent do LD students need to become more capable at speaking in public?)

4. Review the list of questions; revise them and consolidate them accordingly.

5. Place the needs assessment question(s) for the domain, on a Needs Assessment Protocol Worksheet such as seen in Figure 3.1, or another kind of appropriate form.

Figure 3.1: Needs Assessment Protocol Worksheet

<u>**NEEDS ASSESSMENT PROTOCOL WORKSHEET**</u>

Person(s) Formulating the Protocol _____ Date_____

TARGET POPULATION TO BE ASSESSED

NEEDS ASSESSMENT DOMAIN AND QUESTION

STRUCTURE OF NEEDS
<u>CSA</u>   <u>DSA</u>

DATA COLLECTION VARIABLES

DATA COLLECTION METHODS, INSTRUMENTS, PROCEDURES (attach instrumentation to protocol)

METHODS AND PROCEDURES FOR DATA ANALYSIS AND INTERPRETATION

GUIDELINES FOR COMMUNICATION AND USE OF NEEDS ASSESSMENT INFORMATION

ROLES, RESPONSIBILITIES, TIMELINES

6. Repeat steps 1-5 above with the next relevant domain for the target population.

The kinds of needs assessment questions that may be considered appropriate to ask about a target population will vary as a function of the target population, their relevant domains, and relevant context. However, for illustrative purposes, here are a range of *examples* of needs assessment questions that have been appropriately asked and answered in real time situations for various target populations:

Cognitive Domains

- To what extent do behaviorally disordered (BD) high school students need to be proficient at solving social problems?
- In what ways do senior account executives need to learn effective account decision making skills?

Affective Domain

- To what degree do operations associates (OAs) need to learn how to manage their emotions effectively in production situations?
- What affective skills are needed for early childhood special education students to possess to help them succeed in the regular classroom?

Educational Domains

- To what degree do middle school students in the district's western school cluster need to improve language arts skills?
- In what ways do adolescent parents need to increase their basic academic skills?

1.24 Formulate a structure of needs that can guide needs assessment planning

Once appropriate needs assessment questions have been delineated for each relevant domain of the target population, a structure of needs can be formulated for each question within each domain. In essence, a structure of needs is a visual and written description of the discrepancy (need) that is said to exist in a particular domain with respect to the target population. This discrepancy, of course, requires empirical validation as part of a needs assessment. The structure of needs is formulated from the needs assessment question. The structure allows the client, stakeholders, and yourself an opportunity to reflect on the nature and scope of the presumed need and then prepare for measurement and empirical documentation of the extent of the need, as it is structured.

A recommended way to formulate a structure of needs is to describe each presumed discrepancy, qualitatively, as states of affairs – current state of affairs (CSA) and desired state of affairs (DSA) – on the Needs Analysis Protocol Worksheet (Figure 3.1, seen previously), or another kind of form. This can be done in relation to each needs assessment question. The following needs structures, as seen in Table 3.1 below, are real *examples*, for illustrative purposes only:

Table 3.1: Structure of Needs

Needs Assessment Question	CSA	DSA
To what extent do behaviorally disordered (BD) high school students need to be proficient at solving social problems?	BD high school students are not proficient at solving social problems	BD high school students are proficient at solving social problems
To what degree do Operations Associates (OAs) need to learn how to manage their emotions effectively in production situations?	OAs do not know how to manage their emotions effectively during production	OAs know how to manage their emotions effectively during production

When you, your client, and other relevant stakeholders formulate structures of needs, such as the illustrative examples above, it then is possible for all of you to make several *decisions* in further planning of the needs assessment. These decisions are:

1. Whether the need, as structured, is really the area on which needs assessment is usefully focused.

2. Whether the need, as structured, is too general or broad and, therefore, must be segmented; or whether the need statement is too narrow and requires consolidation with other needs assessments.

3. What kinds of operational definitions and variables must be specified for data collection activities with respect to the need (to be discussed as step 1.25 next)?

4. Other decisions.

1.25 Specify variables on which data can be collected to answer each needs assessment question

Once each needs assessment question has been delineated and a structure of needs formulated with respect to that question, it now is possible and appropriate to focus on how the question will be answered. More specifically, attention turns during this step to specifying the variables on which data need to be collected in order to answer the question including defining important terms embedded in the question. With accurate specification of needs assessment data collection variables, the likelihood is increased that reliable and valid evaluative information will be forthcoming. Consequently, more precise direction will be apparent for subsequent program planning and evaluation activities. In this regard, a *data collection variable* is any specific, measurable entity that can be codified or classified having to do with a need, actual or presumed.

Frequently, the data collection variables that are specified during this step become items on instruments such as questionnaires and interview protocols used during the process of determining needs of the target population. To specify meaningful data collection variables, the following procedure has proven practical with clients and relevant stakeholders:

1. State the needs assessment question and/or structure of needs in a clear and concise manner.

2. For each word or phrase in the needs assessment question or needs structure, consider each as a data collection variable; list each variable on a form or the Needs Assessment Protocol Worksheet (see Figure 3.1)

3. Operationalize the variable (define it) so that it is clear to all concerned as to what will be measured.

4. Review the list of data collection variables to decide whether particular variables should be segmented or consolidated.

5. Finalize the list of data collection variables.

Here is an example of an actual list of needs assessment data collection variables, referenced to its structure of needs and needs assessment question:

Table 3.2: A Structure of Need

Needs Assessment Question	CSA	DSA
To What Extent are Elementary School (ES) Teachers Skilled at Participating Effectively as Building Team Members? (Socialization Domain)	ES teachers do not possess Building Team participation skills	ES teachers possess Building Team participation skills

DATA COLLECTION VARIABLES

• Being able to present student referral information (concerns about a student) clearly and specifically to other team members

• Being able to respond to questions from other team members

• Skill at recognizing the opinions and views of other people (both team and non-team members)

• Willingness to receive consultative feedback from team members about referral concerns

1.26 Develop and select methods, procedures, and instruments that will allow data to be collected to answer each needs assessment question

Once data collection variables have been specified for each needs assessment question, program planning and evaluation attention now centers on deciding how to actually gather the data. At this point, therefore, it is necessary to decide upon sound data collection methods, procedures, and instruments. This task involves development of such technology and/or selection of appropriate and available instrumentation.

With respect to this current step, a suggested way to proceed with the client and other stakeholders for each needs assessment question is the following:

1. Review the list of specified data collection variables.

2. For each variable, or cluster of variables, decide about the kind of instrument(s) that can be used to collect the data.

3. With respect to data collection instrumentation, consider one or some combination of the following instruments:

   3.1 Questionnaire—this instrument may be a closed ended instrument, and open ended one, or some combination thereof.

3.2 Interview—this instrument may be a formal (closed ended) interview approach, an informal (open ended) version, or some combination thereof. An interview may also be one to one or in a group format.

3.3 Paper and pencil test—this instrument may be a commercially published one or a noncommercial type. Relatedly, the instrument may be a standardized and norm referenced test, a criterion referenced test, or a context specific version (e.g., teacher made test).

3.4 Rating Scale—this instrument requests a respondent to rate a person with respect to precise scales that are anchored to behaviors or qualities relevant to the person being rated (i.e., as being representative of the target population).

3.5 Applied performance test—this instrument allows for observation and rating of a person with respect to a prescribed task in a naturalistic or simulated setting.

3.6 Checklist—this instrument reflects a list of items to which the respondent is instructed to check for the item's occurrence, non-occurrence, importance, etc.

3.7 Naturalistic observation—this instrument prescribes how behavior or performance of a person is to be observed as it is happening in a real time setting in terms of its frequency, intensity, and/or duration.

3.8 Permanent product review—this instrument prescribes how someone is to review written material relative to a target population, with inferences made about needs, based on analysis.

3.9 Focus group—this instrument reflects use of a group that has the task of focusing on a target population and its need, by means of prescribed format with help of a group facilitator.

4.0 **Other instruments**—as determined by the situation.

4. Select the appropriate instrument, or set of instruments, or develop the instrument, using the following criteria to make instrument selection/development decisions:

4.1 Practicality—the extent to which the instrument can be used by people to gather needs assessment data including the amount of training necessary to appropriately use the instrument.

4.2 Utility—the degree to which the instrument, if used appropriately, will allow the data to be collected that has been specified to be collected and that will serve as an answer to the needs assessment question.

    4.3 Propriety—the manner in which the instrument can be used without violation of any legal or ethical procedures pertinent to the situation.

    4.4 Technical Defensibility—the condition whereby the instrument can be defended in terms of properties of reliability and validity.

5. Place the instruments, methods, and procedures that have been selected and developed into a written sequence such as on the appropriate space on the Needs Analysis Protocol Worksheet (see Figure 3.1), or another suitable form.

6. Develop a sampling approach, if necessary, particularly when the entire target population is known but when it is not possible to assess all of them.

1.27 Specify procedures for analysis and interpretation of needs assessment results

Once methods, procedures, and instruments have been developed and selected for collecting data to answer each needs assessment question, it then is possible and necessary to decide how resulting data will be analyzed and interpreted. Making appropriate data analysis and interpretation decisions helps you, your client, and other stakeholders understand the meaning of the results. Without appropriate analysis and interpretation of needs assessment results, it will not be clear what the collected data means in terms of subsequent program planning and evaluation.

Procedures for needs assessment data analysis and interpretation can be specified in the following way:

1. Decide how the data that will be gathered can be divided and organized in order to meaningfully analyze those results (e.g., by grade level; month of year; corporate division).

2. Decide how the data will be aggregated for data analysis purposes.

3. Decide how aggregated data will be described in terms of descriptive statistics (e.g., central tendency, variability).

4. Decide whether inferential data analyses are necessary to apply with the results; if so, understand why and how to use appropriate inferential statistics (e.g., parametric, non-parametric).

5. Decide the evaluative frames of reference that will be used to interpret the data.
    5.1 Norm referenced
    5.2 Criterion referenced
    5.3 Time series
    5.4 Other

6. Place the data analysis and interpretation decisions that have been made onto the

Needs Assessment Protocol Worksheet (see Figure 3.1), or on another appropriate form.

1.28 Delineate an approach for communication and use of needs assessment information

Once it has been decided how resulting needs assessment data will be analyzed and interpreted, attention then can focus on how information about needs of the target population will be communicated and used for subsequent program planning and evaluation. The task here can be accomplished for each needs assessment question by using the following steps:

1. Delineate what individuals and groups of relevant stakeholders are to receive needs assessment information (e.g., client; teachers; senior executives).

2. Specify exactly what information the identified individuals and groups are to receive (e.g., summary information about percentages of people who meet eligibility criteria across schools).

3. Determine in what forms the information is to be provided:
    3.1 Written report—display tables, graphs, narrative
    3.2 Oral presentation—discussion tables and graphs, etc.

4. Identify the timeline within which the information will be communicated.

5. Describe how people who will receive the needs assessment information will be involved in using it for program planning and evaluation:
    5.1 Needs assessment meeting
    5.2 One to one or small group discussions

6. Based on the above decisions, develop a set of guidelines for communication and use of needs assessment information and place those guidelines in written form on a Needs Assessment Protocol Worksheet (see Figure 3.1), or on another appropriate form.

1.29 Specify needs assessment roles, responsibilities, and timelines

Once a needs assessment has been formulated with respect to a needs assessment question; structure of needs; data collection variables; methods, procedures, and instruments for data collection; and other relevant dimensions as discussed above, it is important to specify how the needs assessment will be implemented. This specification can occur for each needs assessment question. By doing so, the likelihood is increased that the needs assessment will be implemented as planned and useful needs assessment will be implemented as planned and useful needs assessment information will result. Toward that end, the following steps can be taken for each needs assessment question:

1. Delineate the people who will be involved in implementing the needs assessment.

2. Describe the roles that these people will play in needs assessment implementation (e.g., building coordinator, project director, data analyst).

3. Specify the needs assessment responsibilities for the various people that will be fulfilled if the needs assessment is to occur as planned.

4. Set timelines within which the delineated responsibilities and needs assessment activities will occur.

5. Place the above information on a Needs Assessment Protocol Worksheet (see Figure 3.1), or on other appropriate form.

1.30 Place the needs assessment plan into appropriate documents

Once you have thoroughly attended to all the steps described above (1.21 – 1.29), you will have developed a needs assessment protocol for each needs assessment question. If you have used the Needs Assessment Protocol Worksheet (see Figure 3.1), or another appropriate form, you will have complete protocols. Depending on the size of the situation, these protocols can be placed into appropriate documents such as a needs assessment plan document. This kind of document then can be used as a frame of reference for following through on the needs assessment to a successful conclusion.

1.31 Follow through on the needs assessment using needs assessment protocols

The needs assessment protocols can be relied upon in following through on successfully implementing the needs assessment. By using each protocol as a basis for the needs assessment, it is possible to monitor the extent to which the needs assessment has been implemented as planned. In this regard, decisions then can be made about the following matters when following through on the needs assessment:

• Whether particular needs assessment activities are not being implemented.

• Factors that may be inhibiting implementation of these activities; factors that may be facilitating implementation of other activities.

• Revisions that should be made with respect to particular needs assessment activities.

1.32 Construct a needs assessment results document

Once the needs assessment has been completed, it then is possible to determine the needs of the target population that may be addressed by means of a human services program. At this point in the program planning and evaluation process, it is recommended that you place the needs assessment results into a needs assessment results document. Subsequently, following context assessment, the information contained in the needs assessment results document then can be incorporated with context assessment information and relevant target population demographic information into a Clarification Report.

At this point, the needs assessment results document can take the following format:

I. Purpose of the Needs Assessment
II. Description of the Target Population
III. Organization and Client
IV. Structure of Needs
V. Needs Assessment Questions and Answers

1.3 Delineate the Relevant Context

The target population, particularly their psychological and educational needs, do not exist in a vacuum. Rather, they are embedded in a social, cultural, community, and organizational context. This context has implications for the readiness of the target population, the client, relevant stakeholders, and the organization for the design of a human services program that can address important needs. Hence, the relevant context within which the target population and their needs are embedded must be well understood by all concerned if an effective human services program is to be designed and implemented.

Through this third program planning and evaluation activity of the Clarification Phase, the relevant context is delineated. Such context information then serves as another basis for deciding how and when to design and implement a human services program. More specifically, relevant context refers to those factors in the environment of the target population that provide meaning to the target population and their needs and that provide direction for subsequent program planning and evaluation activities.

It is very important to delineate relevant context for several reasons. These reasons are:

- Contextual factors that are likely to facilitate the design and implementation of a program for the target population can be identified. These factors then can be taken into account during the activities of the Program Design phase.

- Contextual factors that may inhibit the design and implementation of a human services program for the target population may be specified. These potentially inhibiting factors then can be considered in terms of how to surmount them during the Program Design phase.

- The readiness of the organization for a human services program for the target population can be judged. In this regard, organizational readiness may suggest the extent to which a program may be designed as well as whether or when it can be implemented according to design.

- Understanding of the relevant context wherein a target population and its needs are embedded allows for precise evaluative judgments to be made about the worth or merit of the program, following its implementation, and, furthermore, enables more accurate projections to be made about implementation of the program in other settings.

- Other reasons.

In order to delineate relevant context within which the needs of the target population are embedded, there are several steps that you can take with the client and other relevant stakeholders. These steps occur within the framework of the A VICTORY approach. In this sense, A VICTORY is an acronym for the first letter of a set of factors about which relevant contextual information can be obtained in a progressive step by step manner with the client and others. (The A VICTORY factors were initially put forth and used by Drs. Howard Davis and Susan Salasin of the National Institute for Mental Health, during the 1970s who were researching factors that contributed to the readiness of community mental health organizations for program evaluation. I have adapted them and utilized them for context assessment factors in relation to program planning and evaluation.)

These steps, therefore, involve consideration of eight (8) A VICTORY factors in conjunction with the client and other relevant stakeholders. These eight factors are listed below:

1.31 Assess the **A**bility of the organization to commit resources to design and implementation of a human services program for the target population.

1.32 Determine the **V**alues that people within the organization and other people who have a stake in the organization ascribe with respect to the target population and its needs, as well as to a human services program.

1.33 Seek to understand **I**deas that people have about the current situation in the organization, with respect to the target population and their needs.

1.34 Determine the **C**ircumstances within the organization that relate to its structure and direction.

1.35 Judge the extent to which the **T**iming of a human services program is appropriate.

1.36 Seek to understand the degree to which organizational members and people who have a stake in it feel **O**bligation to assist the target population by addressing their needs programmatically.

1.37 Make a judgment about **R**esistance that might be encountered by individuals or groups with respect to assisting the target population within the organization.

1.38 Assess the **Y**ield (benefit) that may result for the target population as a consequence of a program as perceived by organizational members.

1.39 Place the relevant context information into a context assessment document.

In any particular situation involving a target population and their needs, it would not be expected that relevant context information will be delineated about all of the above contextual factors, since all of these factors are unlikely to be relevant at any one time. With respect to this third program planning and evaluation activity, though, relevant context refers to information that provides the client, stakeholders, and yourself with direction and validation about whether, how, and when to proceed toward designing a human services program and implementing it, with respect to the target population and their needs.

In delineating the relevant context, one or more of the following context assessment methods can be used. These methods are:

- **Interview**—of key individuals and groups within the organization about the above eight A VICTORY factors and whether these factors, and other ones, may serve to facilitate or inhibit a human services program for the target population.

- **Questionnaire**—designed and used to obtain written responses to questions from people about the above factors and/or other factors.

- **Permanent Product Review**—making judgments and inferences about the context, using the eight factors as a frame of reference, from a review of written materials and data bases.

- **Participant Observation**—judgments and inferences made on your part relative to the above eight factors, based on your involvement and participation with the client and others in the organization.

1.31 Assess the ability of the organization to commit resources to design and implementation of a human services program for the target population

This step is important to undertake since, without adequate resources, it is unlikely that a worthwhile human services program can be designed and implemented. Understanding of the level and extent of resources that the organization is able to commit allows you and the client to make a judgment about what type of program, if any, can be designed. With respect to this step, 'resources' refers to all of the following types: human, technological, informational, financial, physical, and temporal.

Assessment of the organization's "resources ability" can be focused by asking and answering the following questions:

1. What **human resources** can be allotted/dedicated to program design, implementation and evaluation:

   1.1 Managerial/supervisory?
   1.2 Consultants?
   1.3 Staff?
   1.4 Other?

2. What **technological resources** are likely to be available for use in a program:

   2.1 Hardware and software?
   2.2 Methods?
   2.3 Equipment?
   2.4 Validated interventions?
   2.5 Other?

3. What kinds of **informational resources** are available to support program design, implementation, and evaluation:

    3.1 Curriculum guides?
    3.2 Job aids?
    3.3 Checklists?
    3.4 Databases?
    3.5 Other?

4. What **physical resources** can be allotted to the program?

    4.1 Office space?
    4.2 Classroom space?
    4.3 Other?

5. What types and levels of **financial resources** are available for the program:

    5.1 Federal funds?
    5.2 State or local funds?
    5.3 Private funds?
    5.4 Other?

6. How much **temporal resources** can be obtained for the program design, implementation, and evaluation:

    6.1 Days?
    6.2 Weeks?
    6.3 Other?

These questions probably may best be answered by means of interviews with the client and key stakeholders, along with your own observations as a participant in the program planning and evaluation process. Naturally, these questions are not readily answered in a formal, lock step manner. Rather, they typically are answered over time, through a variety of sources, such as those listed above. Often, especially as a program is being designed, additional questions may need to be asked, or the same questions asked again, based on receipt of new information.

1.32 Determine the values that people within the organization and other people who have a stake in the organization ascribe with respect to the target population and its needs, as well as to a human services program

This step is important to undertake since, without an understanding of the values – customs, traditions, beliefs – of the members of the organization, it will be difficult to design a program customized within the organization's culture, addressing needs of the target population. Determining the values of the organization can occur by understanding its members, past and present, particularly in terms of answers to the following questions:

1. What "things" have really mattered traditionally, to the individuals and groups that have comprised the organizations:

    1.1 Professional growth and development?
    1.2 Employment security?
    1.3 Quality service?
    1.4 Other "things"?

2. What have been traditional responses of the organization toward addressing needs of the target population?

    2.1 Very responsive, in a programmatic way?
    2.2 Unaware of their needs?
    2.3 Indifferent to their needs?
    2.4 Other responses?

3. What appears to be the current level of professional commitment of administrators and others within the organization to address the needs of the target population by means of a human services program?

    3.1 Very committed?
    3.2 Unaware of the needs?
    3.3 Somewhat committed, but not a priority commitment?

In following through on this step, it is typically the case that the consultant will be answering these questions and related ones throughout the entire time that they are involved in the program planning and evaluation process with the client. In this regard, however, it is necessary to note here the nature of the answers to these kinds of questions. More specifically, answers to these questions are likely to lead to inferences that you will be making, based on your interviews and from participant observation. Thus, in doing so, it is important not to confuse concomitance with causation in interpreting your answers and in making judgments about organizational values.

1.33 Seek to understand ideas that people have about the current situation in the organization with respect to the target population and their needs

This step is important since, without understanding about how the client, stakeholders and others perceive the "task at hand", the design of a human services program may be incomplete or otherwise misdirected. For this step, the term 'idea' is used in a broad sense as encompassing images and meanings that a current situation has for organizational members and the target population. When you are aware of and understand how people perceive a situation, you are in a more informed position for designing a program and obtaining other pertinent information.

Seeking to understand ideas can occur by asking and answering the following questions, in collaboration with the client:

1. To what extent are people (client, stakeholders, others) clear about what task is to be accomplished (e.g., designing/redesigning a program):

    1.1 Clear?
    1.2 Unaware?
    1.3 Not clear?
    1.4 Indifferent?

2. What do people think is occurring in the organization at the present time with respect to the target population and their needs:

    2.1 Appropriate level of service?
    2.2 Unaware?
    2.3 Too much service?
    2.4 Insufficient service?

3. What does the idea of helping the target population mean to people in the organization:

    3.1 A professional response?
    3.2 A long overdue response?
    3.3 Being directed by outside forces (e.g., state, federal)?
    3.4 Other?

As with determination of values, these questions are probably best answered by means of interview and participant observation procedures.

1.34 Determine circumstances within the organization that relate to its structure and direction

This step is important to undertake in order to obtain an understanding of pertinent and current organizational circumstances. By doing so, it then is possible to be more accurate about how and over what period of time to design a human services program. This is so because you will be aware of the organization's stable features and aspects of the organization that seem to be in flux.

You can make determinations about the organization and its circumstances by asking and answering the following question, in collaboration with the client:

1. How likely is it that the organization's key administrators and other leadership personnel will remain in their current positions?

2. To what extent will the organization's mission and strategic plan remain in force during the next two to three years?

3. How stable has the organization been in terms of its administration, leadership, and personnel?

It is likely that you will be able to obtain information to answer these questions by means of specific permanent product review procedures and by means of specific discussions with the client and also with other relevant stakeholders.

1.35 Judge the extent to which the timing of a human services program is appropriate

This step is important to undertake so that you can make a judgment about whether and to what extent a human services program can be designed, given factors existing at the current time. Knowledge about temporal factors helps in deciding whether the "timing is right" to proceed with a program, including decisions about the nature and scope of a program.

You can make a judgment about whether the timing is right by asking and answering the following questions, again in collaboration with the client:

1. Are key administrators and other relevant stakeholders willing to allow time to be allocated to program design, implementation, and evaluation?

2. To what extent are sources of funding available to support a program (e.g., local, state, federal, private funds)?

3. Do any current events (e.g., elections, new leadership) suggest that the time is appropriate or inappropriate to proceed with program design and implementation?

Once these questions and/or related ones are answered, you then can decide what aspects of the program need to be designed in relation to the specific temporal factors that have been identified.

1.36 Seek to understand the degree to which organizational members and people who have a stake in it feel obligation to assist the target population by addressing their needs programmatically

This step is important to undertake in order to obtain an understanding about people who feel obligated to be involved in subsequent program planning and evaluation activities including program implementation. Understanding about the obligation perceived by people involved in or otherwise affected by the situation and a possible program can help in making particular decisions. These decisions have to do with matters particularly (a) which people need to be involved as active supporters of an initiative; and (b) which people can benefit from more information about the target population and their needs as a basis for enhancing their obligation to the program.

You can better understand the obligation of people to assisting the target population in a programmatic way by asking and answering the following questions:

1. What individuals and groups can be considered as active supporters of a programmatic approach with the target population:

    1.1 Administrators?
    1.2 Staff?

    1.3 Outside Advocates?

    1.4 Peers of the Target Population?

    1.5 Others?

2. What individuals and groups may not support a programmatic initiative with the target population?

Answers to these questions are likely to be obtained by means of interview and possibly from review of written materials.

1.37 Make a judgment about resistance that might be encountered by individuals or groups with respect to assisting the target population within the organization

This step is important to undertake in order to obtain understanding about people who may resist the design and implementation of a program for the target population. Resistance of this kind may be overt and easily observable resistance (e.g., statements made at a meeting) as well as covert and not easily detectable resistance (e.g., lack of attendance at a planning session). Knowledge about people who may resist can help guide program planning activities by using that knowledge to reduce resistance of particular individuals or to avoid involving them in ways that may heighten resistance.

You can obtain information allowing you to make a judgment about resistance by asking and answering the following questions:

1. What individuals or groups are likely to resist a programmatic attempt to address needs of the target population:

    1.1 Administrators?

    1.2 Staff?

    1.3 Outside Advocates?

    1.4 Peers of the Target Population?

    1.5 Other?

2. Over what aspects of a program or other matter may resistance occur:

    2.1 Policies?

    2.2 Program goals?

    2.3 Methods or procedures?

    2.4 Personnel?

    2.5 Budget?

    2.6 Other?

Answers to these questions are most likely to be obtained by means of interview approaches or through judgments made as a result of participant observation procedures.

1.38 Assess the yield (benefit) that may result for the target population as a consequence of a program as perceived by organizational members

This step is important to undertake in order to understand how a program is likely to add value to (a) the target population, (b) program implementers, and (c) the organization. With information about the "payoffs" of program, you are in position to consider how incentive systems and other methods for enhancement of self-motivation can be incorporated into a program's design.

You can obtain information about perceived yield of a program by asking and answering the following questions:

1. What do individuals and groups perceive as benefits of the program:

    1.1 Job enrichment?
    1.2 Professional achievement?
    1.3 Recognition and stature?
    1.4 Target population growth and development?
    1.5 Other?

2. What do individuals and groups perceive as disincentives/drawbacks of a program:

    2.1 Paperwork and related administrative duties?
    2.2 Waste of time, preventing them from engaging in other activities?
    2.3 Program will not be implemented as designed?
    2.4 Other?

Information to answer these questions can be obtained by interview methods and very focused questionnaire approaches.

1.39 Place the relevant context information into a context assessment document

Once the context assessment has been completed at least for the present time, it then is possible to pinpoint contextual factors that are relevant to program design, implementation, and evaluation. At this point in the program planning and evaluation process, it is recommended that you place relevant context information into a written document. This information then can be incorporated with needs assessment results and relevant target population demographic information into a Clarification Report.

In this regard, a context assessment document can take the following format:

    I.   Purpose of the Context Assessment
    II. Description of Target Population
    III. Organization and Client
    IV. Relevant Context Information (by AVICTORY factors)

The next part of this section of the book focuses on the Clarification Report and its purpose, nature, scope, format, and how to construct one.

35

Figure 3.2 is a Context Assessment Protocol Worksheet that can be used to record context assessment information.

Figure 3.2: Context Assessment Protocol Worksheet

CONTEXT ASSESSMENT PROTOCOL WORKSHEET

Person(s) Conducting the Assessment_____ Date_____

Dimension	Method/Procedure	Context Information
Ability of the organization to commit resources		
Values of organizational members		
Ideas of organizational members about the situation		
Circumstances in the organization		
Timing of using a programmatic approach in the organization		
Obligation of individuals and groups		
Resistance expected by individuals and groups		
Yield, or value, of the information and change that may result from a programmatic approach.		

The Clarification Report

The Clarification Report is the name given to a written document that is constructed based on the activities and informational outcomes of the Clarification Phase. Its purpose is to inform the client and other relevant stakeholders about the following elements:

- The nature and scope of a **specified target population**, reflecting demographic and other characteristics that are relevant to needs assessment, context assessment, and other subsequent program planning and evaluation activities.

- The most important **psychological and educational needs** of the target population,

determined by means of needs assessment and that are relevant to context assessment.

- Relevant **context information** related to the target population, **delineated** by means of context assessment and that is relevant for subsequent program planning and evaluation activities.

Based on the information contained in a worthwhile Clarification Report, the client, relevant stakeholders, and yourself as consultant derive one or two of the following benefits:

- Information that provides or otherwise suggests **validation** of a target population, their needs, and relevant context.

- Information that provides or otherwise suggests **direction** for program design, implementation, and evaluation.

A worthwhile Clarification Report is organized by the following sections:

I.   Introductory Information
II. Target Population Description
III. Needs of the Target Population
IV. Relevant Context
*   Appendices I – IV (Professional and Technical Justifications)

I. Introductory Information

The purpose of this section is to provide information that orients or otherwise introduces the reader of the report (e.g., client, stakeholder, consulting group) to (a) the client and (b) the organization in which application of the program planning and evaluation process is to occur.

The information typically is presented in narrative or outline form.

The appendix for this section of the Clarification Report establishes the reason for selecting the particular client and why the organization was described in the way reflected in the report. In most instances, this is not a lengthy section.

II. Target Population Description

The purpose of this section is to provide information about characteristics of the target population that are relevant to the client, stakeholders, and yourself. In this regard, relevancy has to do with information that allows decisions to be made about how to design a program and/or whether to design more than one version of the program.

The information contained in this section will be one of two types:

- Descriptive statistical information that is quantitative in terms of relevant characteristics (e.g., gender, age distributions, frequency counts).

- Narrative information that characterizes the target population in a qualitative way.

This information is likely to be presented in tabular, list, or graphic form supplemented with narrative discussion.

The appendix for this section justifies and defends such decisions and matters as why the population was characterized, quantitatively and qualitatively, the way it has been described, why the population was segmented or not segmented, and other pertinent matters.

III. Needs of the Target Population

The purpose of this section is to provide information about the psychological and educational needs of the target population, described and presented within a discrepancy notion of need.

The information presented may include delineation of needs structures and description of needs in quantitative and qualitative ways. Toward such description, tabular and graphic displays of needs may be useful in informing the client and stakeholders about the needs. This section also outlines the needs assessment questions, data collection variables, and needs assessment methods, procedures, and instruments (more detailed methodological and procedural descriptions can be relegated to the appendix for this section).

The appendix for this section also includes professional and technical justification for all aspects of the needs assessment from selection of questions, data collection variables, instrumentation, procedures for data analysis and other pertinent matters.

IV. Relevant Context

The purpose of this section is to provide information about contextual factors (e.g., AVICTORY dimensions) that indicate readiness of the organization for a program and identify factors that may facilitate or inhibit program design, implementation, and evaluation.

The information presented in this section is likely to be more qualitative and narrative than quantitative, statistical, and tabular in display.

Like the appendix for Section III above, the appendix for this current section includes precise professional and technical justifications.

Appendices

The appendices are referenced to Sections I, II, III, IV, and labeled as such. They offer the client, stakeholders, and others clear, convincing, and cogent rationale for all of the information which is contained in the Clarification Report.

chapter four

DESIGN PHASE

In this chapter, the Design Phase is described in terms of its overarching purpose, constituent activities, technologies, and resulting products.

Purpose of the Design Phase

Without a clear understanding of the human services program that is expected to add value to an individual, group, or organization, it is not possible to make sound judgments about how the program has been implemented or the extent to which the program was worthwhile (i.e., added value to the target population). Lack of clarity about the design of a program (e.g., purpose, goals, activities) sets the conditions for limited understanding about the program, its worth, and how it might be improved or expanded to other sites or settings. This is so because just what is being implemented and evaluated—the program—is not clear to yourself, the client, and other relevant stakeholders. Further, lack of clarity about program design creates a situation where people who are involved with the human services program (e.g. staff, administrators) do not have sufficient guidance or other information to direct them in how to proceed in a timely, economical way. Consequently, these people are likely to become disinterested in doing what is necessary to assure that the program occurs as designed and that desired results are obtained. Alternatively, a program that is designed in a SMART manner (to be discussed) is likely to be implemented and may very well be valuable in terms of target population outcomes. Relatedly, and most importantly, a well-designed program helps to keep the process of program planning and evaluation moving forward in terms of its phases.

The Design Phase is the second of the four major phases of the program planning and evaluation process, the first phase being the Clarification Phase, which has already been discussed in Chapter Three. The purpose of the Design Phase is to document the program in terms of essential program design elements, based on evaluation information from the Clarification Phase as well as the information generated during the Design Phase. This purpose is realized by involving the client, other relevant stakeholders, including a program planning and evaluation team, in gathering, analyzing, and using a range of information. Through Design Phase activities, therefore, a program design is generated that details essential program design elements such as: (a) purpose, goals, and goal indicators; (b) development and implementation schedule; (e) budget; (f) program evaluation plan; and (g) other relevant program design elements. This information is placed into a Program Design Document that serves as a basis for the Implementation Phase and Evaluation Phase of the program planning and evaluation process.

Overview of the Activities of the Program Design Phase

Based on the above purpose, there are four major activities of the Design Phase. These activities are:

2.1 **Describe the program purpose and goals**, so that it will be clear as to what value the program is intended to have.

2.2 **Consider program design alternatives**, in order that a range of methods, procedures, and materials are assessed as being capable of contributing to realization of program purpose and goal attainment.

2.3 **Develop the program**, in terms of having available, or prepared, the important resources that will allow the program to be implemented successfully (i.e., relevant human, technological, informational, financial, temporal, and physical resources).

2.4 **Document the program design**, with respect to its essential elements and in as SMART a manner as possible, thereby increasing the likelihood that the program will be implemented as designed and that it will add its intended value to the target population.

The above four activities are sequential in that one must follow the other for a *well-designed* program to be documented. Further, these activities are interrelated in that the information generated from one activity serves to guide how to proceed with the next activity including the technologies (e.g., methods, materials) to be used as part of the activity. Finally, the activities are reflexive in that changes in one activity and the resulting information may require re-routing to a previously completed activity, in order to modify it.

In the next section of this chapter, the first activity of the Design Phase – Describe the Program Purpose and Goals – is discussed.

2.1 Describe the Program Purpose and Goals

Through this program planning and evaluation activity, the purpose and goals of the human services program are described. Moreover, this description occurs in a way that guides you, the client, and other relevant stakeholders, in deciding exactly how a program is to be designed that can result in those stated outcomes. Further, the purpose and goals of a human services program reflect the value that will be added to the target population by means of the program. Naturally, therefore, without a valuable program purpose and valuable goals that relate to the target population, it is impossible to make decisions about how the target population needs have been addressed and their goals attained. Relatedly, without such information, it will be less likely for you to be able to make evaluative judgments about the degree to which the program has added value to the target population. In fact, without a clearly described program purpose and goals, the entire program design venture can be called into question as a misplaced, inappropriate professional expenditure.

It is very important to describe the purpose and goals of a human services program, for several reasons:

- A statement of program purpose signifies the overall mission and intent of the program. More specifically, this statement provides a capsule summary of *who* is to receive the program, *how* they will be provided it, and *what* value will accrue to them as a result of it. The kind of statement helps communicate the importance of the program with respect to the target population as well as to a range of relevant stakeholders, including funding agents.

- A statement of program purpose helps focus attention of the client, relevant stakeholders, and a program planning and evaluation team on the essence of the program (*who, how, what*). In this way, nonessential information can be deleted or otherwise eliminated from program planning and evaluation routines of these people.

- The goals of a program, if "smartly stated", serve to signify the value of the program and the standards to which all subsequent program planning and evaluation activities are referenced.

- The goals of the program allow a program evaluation plan to be formulated that makes it possible to collect data about the degree of progress of program participants toward each goal and the extent of goal attainment.

- The goals of a program serve as the benchmarks, or targets, in deciding what program technology – methods, materials – and people are to be part of the program.

- The statement of program purpose and goals direct you, the client, and others in deciding whether these outcomes are relevant to the previously described needs of the target population.

In order to describe the purpose and goals of the program, several tasks need to be accomplished by yourself with the client and others, including a program planning and evaluation team if one is being utilized as part of the program planning and evaluation process. These tasks are:

2.11 Review again the needs of the target population and context, in order to assure their accuracy and relevancy.

2.12 Begin formulation of a written statement of program purpose.

2.13 In relation to each need, or set of needs, **S**pecify the valuable accomplishment (goal) in terms of human states, conditions, or qualities.

2.14 For each specified goal (valuable accomplishment), decide how it can be **M**easured.

2.15 Determine whether the specified and measurable goal is **A**ttainable by the people who will participate in the program (target population)?

2.16 Decide whether the specified, measurable, and attainable goal is a **R**elevant one for the target population.

2.17 Delineate a **T**imeframe within which the specified, measurable, attainable, and relevant goal is likely to be attained.

2.18 Formulate a complete version of the program purpose, linked to **SMART** goals.

Each of these tasks will be discussed on the following pages.

2.11 Review again the needs of the target population and context, in order to assure their accuracy and relevancy

Sometimes, the Design Phase is not initiated immediately following the Clarification Phase for any number of reasons, such as school not being in session during the summer months. Consequently, it should not be assumed that the needs of the target population and the relevant context in which those needs are embedded have remained constant. Naturally, a range of developmental, educational, and life related factors could intervene to alter the needs and context pertinent to the target population. Therefore, prior to describing the purpose and goals of the program to be designed, it is advisable to review the needs and context as a "program design security check". If the needs and context have remained the same, then activities of the Design Phase can proceed accordingly. However, if needs and context changes appear evident, then consideration must be given as to whether changes in how to plan and evaluate a human services program are in order and, indeed, whether it may be more appropriate not to move forward with the program planning and evaluation process but rather return to the activities of the Clarification Phase.

The review of needs and context is most important, and it requires neither substantial time nor effort of yourself and the client. Rather, the task can be facilitated by addressing the following questions:

- Are the needs of the target population still current and relevant?

- If yes, how do we know that?

- If no, what evidence leads us to believe that they are not current or relevant (e.g., passage of time such as the summer months)?

- Is the context within which the needs of the target population are embedded still current and relevant?

- If yes, how do we know that?

- If no, what evidence leads us to believe that the context is different?

If needs and context are still current and relevant, program planning and evaluation attention now can shift to the next task.

2.12 Begin formulation of a written statement of program purpose

A statement of program purpose is a written description which informs the reader of that statement about the following:

- **Who** will be provided a human services program as program participants (i.e., the entire target population or some segment of it).

- **How** the program participants will be provided the program in terms of methods, activities, personnel, and location.

- **What** value will accrue to program participants as a result of the program in terms of goals attained, outcomes realized, etc.

As you begin to describe the program's purpose with the client and with others, it will be apparent that you may not be able to complete it as thoroughly as desired. This is so because the activities for the program may not have been decided upon yet (this will occur during Activity 2.2), or the goals have not yet been appropriately stated. Nevertheless, it is helpful to draft an initial program purpose statement, no matter how incomplete it may seem to be, that will be revised and placed in a more complete form later (see task 2.18 below). In doing so, however, remember that the statement always should relate directly to the information in the Clarification Report.

In drafting a written statement of program purpose, it is important to evaluate its completeness. In this regard, criteria for a complete purpose statement about the program are:

1. The statement clearly identifies the people who will participate in the program (**Who**).

2. The statement summarizes the program's technology in terms of the nature and scope of activities that will be implemented and the personnel involved in the program (**How**).

3. The statement delineates the value added to participants through the program in terms of valuable accomplishments such as attainment of program goals (**What**).

Here are examples of actual completed program purpose statements that have served to focus the design of the actual programs:

Example: Statement of Program Purpose for a Performance Appraisal System

Employees for all shifts, at the plant, will participate in the performance appraisal system. Biannually each plant employee will meet with his/her shift supervisor, on a one-to-one basis, to: (a) review the employee's on-the-job performance, using the company's "Goal-Track Pack"; and (b) set goals for the next period. Through this approach, each employee will become knowledgeable about their strengths, as well as their needs for performance improvement, and each employee will collaborate with the shift supervisors in setting important personal work goals for them (employee), during the next period.

Example: Statement of Program Purpose for a Counseling Program

High school students, classified as emotional disturbed, and who are enrolled in the district's special education system, will participate in the program, contingent upon multidisciplinary team verification, parental consent, and an individual student orientation meeting. On a weekly basis during the school year, each participating student will meet with a peer role model who will assist the student in attaining academic achievement levels and socialization skills that are considered by the multidisciplinary team, parents, and the student as normal and school-appropriate. Through this program, students classified as emotionally disturbed will be helped to exit from the special education system.

Example: Statement of Program Purpose for a Personal Development Program

Professional baseball players who are considered by their respective organizations and player agents as being "on-the-brink" of sustained, major league performance will participate in this program, during the off-season, into spring training. With the program consultant and a player personnel specialist/coach, the participants will be involved in a series of group discussions and individual consultation sessions at which they will learn how to design, implement, and evaluate a personal plan of action. As a result of these meetings, the participants will establish precise off-the-field goals that are important to them, as well as to significant others in their lives, and they will take sustained action, throughout the year, toward goals achievement.

2.13 In relation to each need, or set of needs, specify the valuable accomplishment (goals) in terms of human states, conditions, or qualities (KSAs)

Within the context of the program planning and evaluation process, a goal is a statement reflecting a valuable accomplishment, or outcome, which accrues to members of the target population as a result of their participation in a human services program. In this regard, a goal has to do with knowledge (K), skill (S) or ability (A). Relatedly, a goal is derived from a psychological or educational need of the target population, or from a set of needs that combines into a goal statement.

A goal is the basis for subsequent program planning and evaluation activities including activities associated with program design and outcome evaluation. In order to focus these activities in a way that increases the likelihood of a worthwhile human services program, it is useful to consider and understand the requirements of a SMART goal. In this regard, a SMART goal possesses the following properties:

- **S**pecific—the goal statement clearly delineates a valuable accomplishment for the target population in terms of one or more qualities (KSAs) that add value to them and that are linked to their important psychological and educational needs.

- **M**easurable—given the specific goal statement, quantitative indicators are referenced to the goal that guide yourself, the client, and others in deciding to what extent the goal has been attained and how to measure such attainment.

- **A**ttainable—given the needs of the target population and the relevant context, the goal is considered by yourself, the client and knowledgeable others (e.g., subject matter experts) as one that can be realized (attained) by the target population.

- **R**elevant—the goal is considered important, given the needs of the target population, relevant context, and program purpose.

- **T**imeframed—the goal statement is referenced to a particular period of the time within which it is expected to be attained.

This current task involves you, the client, and others in specifying the most important goals to which a program is to be designed. At this point, the task has to do with goal specification in terms of valuable accomplishments. In this regard, valuable accomplishments or outcomes pertinent to the target population have to do with knowledge, skills, and abilities that relate to the states or conditions such as the following:

- Growth
- Development
- Understanding
- Appreciation
- Awareness
- Satisfaction
- Proficiency
- Technical Skill
- Motor Performance
- Daily Living Skill
- Other

As you may realize, the above statements of valuable accomplishments are valuable primarily for reasons intrinsic to an individual, although their existence for particular people may have value for extrinsic purposes such as attainment of organizational goals (productivity, profitability, quality).

Here are *examples* of actual goals from human services programs that embody SMART properties:

An Example Goal Statement with SMART Properties
(extracted from the Performance Appraisal System example above)

Plant employees will understand their on-the-job performance strengths and their performance areas in need of improvement, based upon information communicated to them during their performance review meetings with their shift supervisors.

- At one month, three month, and six month time intervals following performance review meetings, random samples of plant employees will be asked to complete the "Performance Development Survey" (which is a structured questionnaire that measures employee understandings about their on-the-job performance and what it means for improvement).

- It is anticipated that, for each sample, 80-90% of the employees will be able to state their understandings accurately, in accordance with supervisor understandings.

An Example Goal Statement with SMART Properties
(extracted from Counseling Program example above)

Emotionally disturbed (ED) student participants will achieve passing grades in regular education academic classes in which they are enrolled, during the first school semester (at the semester's conclusion, all grades in all regular education academic classes will be compiled by the program director).

- It is anticipated that, for ED student participants, the following results will obtain:
  o 60-70% will obtain C grades or higher in all courses.
  o 5-10% will obtain D grades or less in all courses.

2.14 For each specified goal (valuable accomplishment), decide how it can be measured

In order to measure (i.e., obtain data on) each specified goal, it is necessary that goal indicators be identified and that these indicators be considered as valid relative to the goal. In this regard, a goal attainment indicator is one which can be measured in some practical way and that allows one to make a judgment that the goal was attained or that progress is being made by the target population toward the goal.

In order to decide what valid goal indicators are, and in order to distinguish between a goal and a goal indicator, the following perspectives have proven to be important for those involved in the program planning and evaluation process:

1. A goal is a valuable accomplishment that is intrinsic to the program participants (target population). For instance, the goal, "To develop reading comprehension ability," is intrinsically valuable to the program participants in that, if the goal is attained, each participant will be more valuable to himself or herself in that they now will be able to acquire new information, retain it, and use it to function more effectively in society. Similarly, the goal, "To develop awareness of ones strengths and needs as a supervisor," also is intrinsically valuable to a supervisory target group. Likewise, the goal, "To develop effective listening skills," is a valuable accomplishment, intrinsic in nature, and potentially useful to the people who are involved in a human services program (e.g., conduct disordered adolescents; sales people).

2. In each of the above three examples, you do not actually see the goals. More specifically, in the forms stated above, you are not able to proceed directly to measure each goal since there is no indicator of what data are to be collected, when

and what criterion signify goal attainment. This is so because the goal statement denotes something that is valuable, an accomplishment, but that is intrinsic in importance.

3. A goal indicator is a measure that allows you, the client, and others to make a judgment about goal attainment. In this sense, a goal indicator is something that (a) can be observed and agreed upon as a valid indicator of the goal, (b) can be measured by means of an appropriate instrument, method, or procedure, and (c) has only extrinsic importance, solely as a way of making a judgment about the intrinsic goal. In essence, a goal indicator allows the following questions to be answered:

- Who will be measured with respect to progress toward the goal or goal attainment (e.g., target population member(s))?

- What will be measured with respect to the goal (e.g., knowledge, skill, ability, attitude)?

- How will measurement occur (e.g., test, checklist, observation, permanent procedure)?

- When will measurement occur (e.g., daily, pre-program, post-program) and by whom (e.g., teacher, consultant)?

- What standards or criteria will signify desired levels of goal attainment?

Here are actual examples of goals that have goal indicators referenced in them:

An Example Goal Statement with SMART Properties
(extracted from the Performance Appraisal Systems example above)

Plant employees will understand their on-the-job performance strengths and their performance areas in need of improvement, based upon information communicated to them during their performance review meetings with their shift supervisors.

- At one month, three month, and six month time intervals following performance review meetings, random samples of plant employees will be asked to complete the "Performance Development Survey" (which is structured questionnaire that measures employee understandings about their on-the-job performance and what it means for improvement).

- It is anticipated that, for each sample, 80-90% of the employees will be able to state their understandings accurately, in accordance with supervisor understandings.

An Example Goal Statement with SMART Properties
(extracted from Counseling Program example above)

Emotionally Disturbed (ED) student participants will achieve passing grades in regular education academic classes in which they are enrolled, during the first school semester (at the semester's conclusion, all grades in all regular education academic classes will be compiled by the program director).

- It is anticipated that, for ED student participants, the following results will obtain:
  o 60-70% will obtain C grades or higher in all courses.
  o 5-10% will obtain D grades or less in all courses.

In deciding how each goal can be measured by means of goal indicators, it is helpful for you to consider each goal indicator in relation to four qualities, before selecting and finalizing the indicator.

These qualities are:

1. **Practicality**—The goal indicator is one on which data can be collected without disruption to operational routine of the organization.

2. **Utility**—If data are collected with respect to the goal indicator, the resulting information can be used in making valid judgments about goal attainment.

3. **Propriety**—The goal indicator adheres to all pertinent legal strictures and ethical standards.

4. **Technical Soundness**—The goal indicator can be defined in terms of relevant dimensions of reliability and validity.

If a goal indicator cannot be justified because it does not possess one or more of the above qualities, it should not be linked to a goal.

2.15 Determine whether the specified and measurable goal is attainable by the people who will participate in the program (target population)

Once each goal has been specified and one or more appropriate goal indicators referenced to it, attention then can turn to deciding whether the goal can be attained by the target population. In making this decision, it usually is necessary to consider the time frame for the program and goal, which will be discussed below. However, attainability also needs to be considered in its own right, since it is an important psychological dimension.

There are several steps that you can take with the client and other stakeholders in considering the attainability of a goal relative to the target population. These steps are:

1. Review the goal statement, its indicator, and time frame as necessary. If these are not clear, they must be clarified before proceeding. Otherwise, goal attainability will be impossible to judge in a precise sense.

2. For each goal that is specific, measurable, and time framed, identify and discuss the range of evidence which exists that leads you to think that the goal can be attained by the target population. In this regard, such evidence may take one or more of the following forms:

- Results from program evaluations where the same or similar program was implemented with a like target population.

- Reactions of the target population to similar goals in the recent (within 12 months) past.

- Testimonials and opinions from other professionals who have said that they have helped a like target population attain the goal.

- Advice and counsel of respected subject matter experts.

- Your own professional judgments, based on your prior experience with similar goals and like target populations.

- Other evidence.

3. For each goal, consider the following dimensions of perceived attainability for the target population:

   - **Goal Understanding** – this refers to the extent that the target population is able to understand what the goal means to them as a valuable, intrinsic accomplishment.

   - **Goal Prerequisites** – this refers to whether the target population already possesses knowledge and skill that are thought necessary as a basis for attaining the goal.

   - **Goal Desire** – this refers to whether the target population is likely to be emotionally invested in wanting to attain the goal.

4. Based on discussions of exiting evidence (step number two) and consideration of attainability (step number three), you may be directed in one or more of the following ways with respect to the goal:

   - **Evidence** and **perceived attainability** may be sufficient to judge that the goal can be attained.

   - **Evidence** may not exist that allows a judgment that the goal has a reasonable chance of being attained. In such an instance, the goal may require further specification, alternative measurement, a different time frame, or eliminated as a part of the program's design.

   - If **goal understanding** is judged low for the target population, consideration needs to be given to how such understanding may be increased as part of the program design.

- If **goal prerequisites** are judged insufficient for the target population, the members of it may need a remedial or complementary program prior to their participation in the current one.

- If **goal desire** seems low for the target population, the program design may need to incorporate specific motivational methods.

5. If evidence exists and perceived attainability is high, the goal can be considered a reasonable one for inclusion in the program with respect to goal attainment.

2.16 Decide whether the specified, measurable, and attainable goal is a relevant one for the target population

To this point, each goal has been specified, a way of measuring it considered, and a judgment made that each goal has a reasonable chance of being attained by the target population. Now, it is important to make sure that the goal is relevant to the target population as well as to the mission of the organization wherein a human services program is to be designed and implemented.

With respect to the target population, a goal can be considered relevant if it possesses several features. These features are:

1. Reflects a valuable accomplishment for each person having to do with knowledge, skill, or ability.

2. The valuable accomplishment is intrinsic to the worth of each person and serves as a means to other valuable accomplishments.

3. The valuable accomplishment is proper and appropriate to society.

With respect to the organization, a goal for the target population can be considered relevant if it aligns with the overall mission of the organization.

2.17 Delineate a timeframe within which the specified, measurable, attainable, and relevant goal is likely to be attained

Naturally, it takes time to have a human services goal attained. Unfortunately, in many instances of program planning and evaluation, the time that it is likely to take for a goal to be attained is not really considered, nor framed, by those involved in the process. This current task is part of the Design Phase solely to assure that time is considered in an explicit way by yourself, the client, and relevant stakeholders.

In delineating a **frame of time** within which it is likely that a human service goal can be attained, there are a set of separate, yet interrelated questions that can be addressed for each goal. These questions are:

1. What prior program evaluation data exists that suggests the amount of time it will take for goal attainment?

2. What do the identified needs indicate about the time it will take for goal attainment?

3. What is suggested by the relevant context that suggests an appropriate timeframe for goal attainment?

4. What informed opinions can be obtained (e.g., from subject matter experts) about the goal and time related factors?

By considering these questions and answering them, understanding will be increased about the time it will take to attain a particular goal. Relatedly, such understanding will help you make a judgment about the "degree of certainness" that you have about time and the particular goal. Whatever the situation, delineation of a timeframe that is linked to each human service program goal is a most important part of this initial activity of the Design Phase.

2.18 Formulate a complete version of the program purpose, linked to SMART goals

At this point, it is useful to make sure that each program goal is as SMART as possible and that each SMART goal is directly relevant to the statement of program purpose. Thus, this current task is devoted to placing program purpose and goals into a complete form, as a basis for the Design Phase's second activity (2.2), Consider Program Design Alternatives, discussed next.

2.2 Consider Program Design Alternatives

Before engaging productively in this second activity of the Design Phase, when various ways that a program can be designed are considered, it is necessary now to introduce and discuss several major programmatic concepts. Without thorough understanding of these concepts, the human services program may be designed in an incomplete manner. These major concepts are: (a) program design, (b) program design elements, and (c) program design document.

Program Design

Just like a house or car has a fundamental design, so does a program. In order to build a house or car, or to redesign those objects, the architect or engineer requires clear understanding of the objects' design and accurate documentation with respect to its essential elements. Without such information, it would not be possible to undertake, in a professional way, the design or redesign of the house or car. While, upon reflection, such fundamentals seem obvious, it is not surprising to observe the relatively little focused and professional attention given to the design of a human services program as a part of the program planning and evaluation process; often, the program's design is considered in a cavalier way or more typically not at all. Consequently, it then is not surprising to observe a program that cannot be successfully implemented when it has a poor design or no design whatsoever.

A program design reflects the structure of a program with respect to its most important elements (to be discussed shortly). The design of a program has one primary focus or reference point and that is the description of the program purpose as well as the SMART goals that are linked to that purpose. The program design is formulated, or reformulated, only following description of program purpose and goals. If a program is designed without such a reference point, an incomplete program will be implemented.

Program Design Elements

A human services program's design encompasses a range of elements. In this regard, it is these elements that give the program form and substance and provide the direction for how the program is to be developed and implemented. Although the specific form and substance of each program design element will vary depending on the purpose and goals of a particular program, the following are program design elements that are typical of human services programs:

1. Basic Reference Point – statement of Program **Purpose and SMART Goals**.

2. **Eligibility Standards and Criteria**, that indicate what members of the target population can participate in the program.

3. **Policies and Procedures**, that guide program personnel in how to function within the program.

4. **Methods and Techniques**, that are used by program personnel with participants as a means to facilitate goal attainment.

5. **Materials**, that are used in conjunction with the methods and techniques.

6. **Equipment**, that helps support program operations.

7. **Facilities**, in which the program is implemented.

8. **Components, Phases, and Activities**, that delineate the process of the program and how it will be implemented.

9. **Budget**, that also supports program operations.

10. **Personnel**, who are responsible for implementation of the program.

11. **Incentives**, which help set the conditions so that program personnel and participants will want to follow through on the Program.

12. **Program Evaluation Plan**, that allows data to be gathered and analyzed so that judgments of worth and merit can be made about the Program.

Each of these program design elements is described in detail under Activity 2.4, Document the Program Design, to be discussed shortly.

Program Design Document

This is a written description of the essential elements of the program that serves as the basis for the Implementation Phase and the Evaluation Phase of the program planning and evaluation process. The program design document will be discussed in detail under Activity 2.4.

Tasks Associated with Program Design Activity 2.2, Consider Program Design Alternatives

In order to consider alternatives that may be appropriate for incorporation into the design of a human services program, a set of particular tasks have proven useful. By completing these tasks in the appropriate way, the chances are reduced that you, the client, and others will not get "locked into" any non-customized set of alternatives. Rather, the likelihood is increased that a program will be designed that is customized to the needs of the target population and to the purpose and goals of the program.

The tasks to be completed as part of this activity of the Design Phase are the following:

2.21 Review again the statement of purpose and goals of the program.

2.22 Determine whether eligibility standards and criteria and/or policies need to be stated for the program.

2.23 For each goal, or set of goals, consider whether a separate program component or phase is warranted.

2.24 For each component or phase, consider the methods, techniques, procedures, materials and other elements that can comprise it.

2.25 For each component or phase, consider the personnel who can be associated with it.

2.26 Sequence the program components or phases.

2.27 Specify a budget that will support program development and program implementation.

2.28 Formulate a program evaluation plan.

2.21 Review again the statement of purpose and goals of the program

There may be situations when the program is designed at a date far removed from the time the purpose of the program was started and goals formulated. These situations may have to do with matters such as: (a) delays in receipt of the authorization for funding, (b)

53

unexpected resistance to the program, resulting in a decision not to proceed with further program design activities, (c) summer months or holidays, and (d) other reasons. In these situations, it is important to determine whether the purpose and goals still are appropriate. It is important to do so before proceeding with considering program design alternatives. Otherwise, the alternatives being considered may not be current or relevant, given existing conditions.

This task can be completed by asking and answering the following question in conjunction with the client and others including the program planning and evaluation team:

- To what extent are the program's purpose and goals still current and relevant?

If the answer to the question is that they still are current and relevant, then attention can turn to the next task. If not, changes need to be made in purpose and/or goals before proceeding.

2.22 Determine whether eligibility standards and criteria and/or policies need to be stated for the program

A human services program's design and implementation will be enhanced with particular kinds of information that guides and directs people associated with it. These people include individuals responsible for administration of the program, people who will implement it, and other stakeholders. In this regard, the task at hand for you, the client, and others is whether the program's design can benefit from the following information:

- Eligibility standards and criteria
- Policies

Eligibility Standards and Criteria

Eligibility standards and criteria relate directly to the target population, their needs, and their relevant demographic characteristics. In essence, eligibility standards and criteria are written statements that inform people associated with the program about who is eligible to participate in it. Not all human services programs require explicit, written eligibility standards and criteria, especially those programs that are customized to a particular group at a specific site. However, programs that receive state and federal funds and/or are regulated by public agencies typically require statements about eligibility of individuals for the program as public assurances that the appropriate people are being provided it.

Here are actual examples of statements of eligibility standards and criteria for various kinds of human services programs.

An Example from a Counseling Program

A student is eligible to participate in the program if he/she meets the following standards and criteria:

- Is classified as severely behaviorally disordered, pursuant to state special education regulations.

- Has participated in the program's orientation session.

- Possesses documented need in accordance with the determined needs of the target population.

- Has written permission of a parent/guardian.

An Example from a Workplace Literacy Program

A worker at the main plan can participate in the program if he/she meets the following conditions:

- Obtains a score of lower than the 20th percentile with respect to "general worker norms" of the Adult Basic Learning Examination (ABLE).

- Agrees to an individualized workplace learning analysis including educational achievement testing.

- Receives scheduling permission from departmental supervisors.

Policies

Policies relate to important matters of how a program is to operate. As a written statement, a policy reflects practical wisdom about one or more aspects of a human services program. Moreover, a policy statement is important for program planning and evaluation to the degree that it helps you, the client, and others (e.g., program implementers) understand (a) who can be provided the program, (b) how they can receive it, and (c) what can be expected from the participants following their entry into the program.

Here are two actual examples of policy statements from two different programs:

An Example from a Performance Appraisal System

Each employee in the plant is to meet, on an annual basis, with his/her shift supervisor, to review on the job performance.

An Example from a Counseling Program

Only ED students who meet all criteria for entrance into the program can participate in it.

With respect to determining the necessity of written statements of eligibility standards and criteria and/or policies for the program's design, several questions can be considered by yourself, in concert with the client and other people (e.g., program design team). These questions are:

1. Will the written statement (e.g., standard policy) be able to be adhered to by professionals and participants?

2. Will the written statement inform professionals and participants about how to proceed?

3. Will the written statement respect the rights of people and all relevant ethical and legal concerns?

If answers to these questions are in the affirmative, it is likely that each written statement will be a valuable addition to the design of the program.

2.23 For each goal, or set of goals, consider whether a separate component or phase is warranted

At this point in the Design Phase of the program planning and evaluation process, goals have been described that are derived from the program's statement of purpose and that are in SMART form. In many programs, these goals are parts of larger domains such as: (a) cognitive or knowledge domains, (b) psychomotor or skills domains, or (c) attitudinal or ability domains. This current task has to do with considering whether one or more of the goals can be grouped together in a way that a separate program component or program phase can be linked to it.

A program component or phase can be considered as a "mini program," within the larger program design. In this regard, a program component (phase) is distinguished in the following way:

1. It (i.e., the component or phase) is focused on a particular goal or set of goals that share common characteristics (e.g., knowledge, or skill, or abilities).

2. It (component or phase) encompasses a distinct set of programmatic resources. These resources, which will be discussed in more detail under Program Design Tasks 2.24 to 2.27, may include the following ones:

    • Methods and Techniques
    • Materials
    • Activities (sequenced progressively over time)
    • Equipment
    • Facilities
    • Budget
    • Personnel
    • Incentives

In deciding whether a program goal, or set of goals, warrants a separate component or phase, the following questions can be considered:

    • Does the goal(s) relate to a larger domain (e.g., knowledge development) that is distinct from other domains that overarch particular program goals (e.g., skill acquisition, attitude development)?

- Does the goal(s) demand a substantial amount of time to be attained and a particular technological approach (e.g., lecture vs. role playing)?

- Does attainment of the goal(s) serve as a prerequisite for attainment of other goals in other domains?

- Other questions.

If answers to all or most of the above questions are in the affirmative, it probably is important to consider a separate component or phase.

2.24 For each component or phase, consider the methods, techniques, procedures, materials, and other elements that comprise it

Each component (or phase) of a human services program can be thought of as a mini program or a program unto itself. Naturally, if there is more than one component, there must be information available as part of the program design to direct the people associated with the program (e.g. administrator, implementer) about just how the components are coordinated.

For each component (phase), it is important at this point to consider a range of elements that might comprise that component. A set of elements that can be considered together for a component are the following:

- Methods, Techniques, Procedures
- Materials, Forms, Checklists
- Equipment, Tools
- Incentives (Monetary and Nonmonetary)
- Facilities, Other Resources

These elements are discussed below.

Methods, Techniques, Procedures

A *method* is a particular way of doing something as part of a program, according to some convention, best practice, curriculum guide, or plan. A method involves the knowledge of the person using the method as to why it is being used along with any skill required by the person in using the method. For instance, naturalistic observation of students in a classroom or workers in an office is a method of gathering data about behaviors and activities of individuals and groups. Also, role playing is a method of teaching participants in a group counseling program about how to behave in a certain role and in a certain context, as basis for trying out the behavior in a real time setting.

A *technique* is distinguished from a method in that the technique is a specific and prescribed way of performing the mechanical details of a skill. In this sense, a technique reflects the performer's technical skill as part of a program such as the technique of encouraging a counselee to express their opinions about a difficult issue or subject. A method typically encompasses a set of interrelated techniques.

When considered within a program design context, a *procedure* is a way for the program implementer to proceed in doing things, as part of the program. For instance, there may be a procedure for orienting participants to a program prior to their participation in it.

Examples from a Performance Appraisal System

- **Method**—using a written handout to orient the employee to the meeting and its purpose

- **Technique**—"reflecting back", to the employee, the supervisor's interpretation of the employee's opinion about their own performance

- **Procedures**—orienting the employee to the meeting, then giving the employee a copy of the results

Examples from a Counseling Program

- **Method**—using a videotape about positive anger control

- **Technique**—getting the counselee to attend to the videotape and rate the "actor's performance"

- **Procedure**—introducing the video, showing it, rating it, discussing it, relating the video content to "real-life" concerns of counselee

Materials, Forms, Checklists

Materials are the books, tapes, manuals, software, worksheets, and other products that are used by program personnel and participants during a program. While it may be obvious as to the nature of the materials used in a program, that which may not be so obvious however is: *who* the materials are for; *how* the materials are to be used, and *what* is expected to happen/result from the materials utilization. More specifically in considering materials for a program, the following questions can be addressed:

- **Who** is the material targeted to?
  - o All of the target population?
  - o Some of the population?
  - o Personnel?

- **How** is the material to be used?
  - o Frequency?
  - o Intensity?
  - o Duration?
  - o Condition?

- **What** is expected to happen when the material is used?
  - o Anticipated reactions of user (e.g., affective, physical, social)?
  - o Contributions to learning (e.g., preprogram, during program, , post program)?
  - o Practical for use?

Forms and *checklists* are the printed matter that allows data to be collected, as a basis for decisions about the program. While it, too, may be obvious as to the nature and scope of the forms and checklists that constitute a program, it is helpful when the following question about forms and checklists can be addressed:

- **Who** is to use the form(s) or checklist(s) and for what **purpose**?

- **How** is the form(s) or checklist(s) to be used and what **training** is necessary to assure that it/they are used correctly and reliably?

- **What** is expected to happen as a result of using the form(s) or checklist(s) in terms of **program action**?

Equipment, Tools

Equipment and *tools* represent hardware and related devices that are instrumental in operation of the program and that will contribute, if used properly, to program effectiveness. Equipment and tools need to meet particular specifications, in order to be considered as being of appropriate quality and, hence, suitable for use as part of a program. Equipment and tools need to be used with respect to particular methods, for specific reasons.

Incentives (Monetary and Nonmonetary)

An *incentive* can be considered as that thing or entity which appears to urge people – program participants, personnel – to action/accomplishment. An incentive also may be termed a motive, stimulus, or cause of action. A *monetary incentive* (e.g., incentive pay, bonus) is a payment to induce workers to increase or improve production. A *nonmonetary incentive* is a non-wage tangible product or intangible element that induces a worker to perform in a prescribed way.

Facilities, Other Resources

Facilities have to do with building, rooms, and other places wherein a program will operate. Other resources refer to additional sources of information, expertise, energy, or electrical power needed for the program to be effective.

2.25 For each component or phase, consider the personnel who will be associated with it

There are various ways to consider the personnel who will be associated with a component or phase of a human services program. All of these ways are important to consider in order to prevent making personnel decisions too quickly and, hence incompletely or erroneously, in program design. In this regard, personnel can be considered in terms of the "3 Rs":

- **R**ole—the part or function a person is to perform with respect to the program or component (phase), including major job accomplishments.

- **R**esponsibilities—the specific tasks or activities assigned to the person.

- **R**elationships—the manner in which the person is to relate to other people associated with the component (phase) or to the overall program.

Role

A role is a major part or function an individual is asked to play. In this sense, a person may play one or more roles. Examples include:

- **Administrator** of the program (and component).
- **Supervisor** of the personnel who function within the component.
- **Consultant** to personnel within the component.
- **Direct services provider** within the component (e.g., teacher, counselor).
- **Evaluator** of the worth or merit of the component, following its implementation.
- Other possible roles.

With respect to one's role in a component, phase, or overall program, it is important to be able to identify the major accomplishments of individuals who perform successfully in the role. Typically, personnel roles are linked to job descriptions and not to particular programs. Further, roles usually are not referenced to role accomplishments for the program. This situation becomes problematic in program design where it is important to understand how personnel are to function, what is expected of them (role accomplishments), and then to communicate the information to involved personnel.

Role accomplishments have to do with outcomes or results expected of the individual from playing a certain role with respect to a human services program. Role accomplishments can be thought of as the products or evidence that exists once the individual playing the role leaves the program setting. Naturally, as is the case with all program design elements, roles and role accomplishments are based on, indeed derived from, the program's purpose and goals as well as needs of the target populations. As such, role accomplishments would be such things as:

- Educated program participants
- Completed reports
- Quality innings pitched
- Claims processed
- Inspections conducted
- Programs evaluated
- Students counseled
- Components designed
- Lessons taught
- Other role accomplishments

Naturally, for each program component and program design, the particular roles and role accomplishments can be described in more pertinent detail with empirical indicators attached to them.

Responsibilities

A responsibility is a specific task or activity assigned to a person as part of their role in the component or overall program. Typically, someone associated in a professional or paraprofessional role with a program or program component has several associated responsibilities. Often, these responsibilities are embodied in a job description. *General examples* of responsibilities that are related to various roles are the following:

Administrator Role
* Monitor participant progress
* Complete program reports
* Appraise personnel performance

Supervisor Role
* Observe on the job performance
* Provide feedback on performance to supervisors
* Coach employees toward exemplary performance

Consultant role
* Define problems and opportunities with the program client
* Listen to programmatic concerns of the client
* Communicate results of consultation transactions

Direct Service Provider Role
* Instruct students in socialization skills
* Confer with parents on progress of their children
* Assist students who have remedial learning needs
* Other responsibilities, referenced to a particular role

Here, too, the responsibilities of program personnel are specified in more detail with regard to a component or phase of a human services program.

Relationships

Within the context of program design, a relationship is the manner in which one person associated with a component interacts with and otherwise communicates with other people associated with the entity. More specifically, program relationships have to do with the following kinds of transactions, as examples of the larger universe of possible program relationships:

* **Administrator** of a district program with a professional from the corporate office.

* **Supervisor** with his or her *supervisees* in terms of performance appraisal and feedback.

61

- **Consultant** with a program *implementer* about how to redesign a part of a program.

- **Direct service provider** with program *participants* with respect to one to one counseling of them.

- Other program relationships.

For each program component, of course, every program relationship requires specification so that all parties concerned with the program can understand its parameters.

2.26 Sequence the program components or phases

When a program has been implemented, and someone observes it, "what" one typically sees is characterized as activities (i.e., what people do, and how they do it). Activities of a program often are sequenced within a component, progressively; program activities occur in a planned, purposeful sequence. Activities, as they occur as part of a component or phase, occur over a particular period of time. Effective programs, therefore, are ones that reflect activities which are sequenced and timed in planned, purposeful ways, by component or phase, often by visual means such as with flow charts or procedural guides.

2.27 Specify a budget that will support program development and implementation

In some way, a budget is attached to a program, and there are many ways to develop a system of costs that can be program-oriented/referenced. In terms of the program planning and evaluation process, the estimation of costs for a program budget can be organized in terms of costs for clarification costs, program design costs, implementation costs, and outcome evaluation costs.

The "worksheets" below contain a few formulas that make it easier to consider and estimate program costs, for budget purposes, for a particular human services program (NB: all formulas and areas may not be relevant to a particular program).

Figure 4.1: Budget Worksheets

Clarification Costs	
Salaries and Employee Benefits – Staff	_____
Meals, Travel, Incidental Expenses	_____
Office Supplies and Expenses	_____
Consultation Services	_____
Equipment Expenses	_____
Other Relevant Costs	_____
Total Clarification Costs	

Program Design Costs	
Salaries and Employee Benefits – Staff	_____
Meals, Travel, Incidental Expenses	_____
Office Supplies and Expenses	_____
Program Materials and Supplies	_____
Training Expenses	_____
Equipment Expenses	_____
Facilities Costs	_____
General Overhead Allocation	_____
Other Costs	_____
Total Program Design Costs	_____

Program Implementation Costs	
Participant Costs (salary and benefits)	_____
Program Material and Supplies	_____
Participant Replacement Costs	_____
Lost Production	_____
Instructor Costs	_____
Salaries and Benefits	_____
Meals, Travel, Incidental Expenses	_____
Facility Costs	_____
Other Costs	_____
Total Implementation Costs	_____

Outcome Evaluation	
Salaries and Employee Benefits – Staff	_____
Meals, Travel, Incidental Expenses	_____
Office Supplies	_____
Printing and Reproduction	_____
Consulting Services	_____
Equipment Expenses	_____
Data Analyses Expenses	_____
Other Costs	_____
Total Evaluation Costs	_____
Total Program Costs	_____

2.28 Formulate a program evaluation plan

An essential, albeit usually absent, program design element is a clear, concise, written plan to evaluate the program. A program evaluation plan enables program personnel to gather data, in response to particular evaluation questions, and to use the evaluation information for judging the program's worth/merit and for making subsequent program planning decisions. A program evaluation plan details the following:

- Evaluation Questions
- Data Collection Variables

- Methods, Instruments, Procedures for Data Collection
- Methods and Procedures for Data Analysis and Interpretation
- Guidelines for Communicating Evaluation Results

2.3 Develop the Program

Through this program planning and evaluation activity, the design of the human services program is actually *developed* into a form that is ready for implementation, when required and as designed. This third activity of the Design Phase often is overlooked, given incomplete attention, or addressed in a less than systematic and thorough way by professionals associated with the program planning and evaluation process. Consequently, under such lack of focused circumstances, it is not surprising that the human services program is not implemented as designed.

It is very important to *develop* a human services program for several reasons:

- A considerable investment of time and other resources already has occurred with respect to the program and with respect to the program planning and evaluation process (i.e., the Clarification Phase; the first two activities of the Design Phase). This investment of time and other resources can be maximized through a sound approach to program *development*.

- The activity of *developing* the program helps assure that the attention of yourself, the client, and a program planning and evaluation team centers on the precise details seen as important to assure program implementation success and worthwhile program outcomes.

- Through a procedurally detailed approach to program *development*, obstacles to successful implementation not already identified are likely to become apparent. This is so because, in order *develop* the program appropriately and according to design, attention to detail is paramount.

- The "readiness for implementation" of a thoroughly *developed* human services program then can be very accurately assessed just prior to the time of implementation.

In order to *develop* the human services program, several tasks need to be accomplished by yourself with the client and others, including the program planning and evaluation team, if one is being used as part of the program planning and evaluation process.

These tasks are:

2.31 Develop the program's **human resources**
2.32 Develop the program's **technological resources**
2.33 Develop the program's **informational resources**
2.34 Develop the program's **financial resources**
2.35 Develop the program's **physical resources**
2.36 Develop the program's **temporal resources**

The Program Development Matrix

An essential device for *program development* is the Program Development Matrix as seen in Table 4.1. The Program Development Matrix consists of two major dimensions. These dimensions are:

- **Program Design Elements**—seen as the vertical dimension of the Matrix, representing the essential elements of the human services program as previously described in this book.

- **Resource Dimensions**—seen as the horizontal dimension of the Matrix, representing the range of the resources that may need to be developed for a particular human services program.

The juxtaposition of the vertical dimension of the Program Development Matrix with the horizontal dimension forms 72 matrix cells. These cells help guide decisions about what needs to be developed for a particular program as seen in terms of the following six tasks (2.31 – 2.36).

Table 4.1: Program Development Matrix

Program Design Elements	Human (H)	Technological (TE)	Informational (I)	Financial (F)	Physical (P)	Temporal (TM)
1. Purpose and SMART Goals	H1	TE1	I1	F1	P1	TM1
2. Eligibility Standards and Criteria	H2	TE2	I2	F2	P2	TM2
3. Policies and Procedures	H3	TE3	I3	F3	P3	TM3
4. Methods and Techniques	H4	TE4	I4	F4	P4	TM4
5. Materials	H5	TE5	I5	F5	P5	TM5
6. Equipment	H6	TE6	I6	F6	P6	TM6
7. Facilities	H7	TE7	I7	F7	P7	TM7
8. Components, Phases, and Activities	H8	TE8	I8	F8	P8	TM8
9. Budget	H9	TE9	I9	F9	P9	TM9
10. Personnel	H10	TE10	I10	F10	P10	TM10
11. Incentives	H11	TE11	I11	F11	P11	TM11
12. Program Evaluation Plan	H12	TE12	I12	F12	P12	TM12

2.31 Develop the program's human resources

This task involves use of the Human Resources Dimension of the Program Development Matrix in relation to each element of the Program Design Elements Dimension of the Matrix. In this regard, various questions can help identify the specific "human resource program development tasks" that need to be accomplished in order for the human services program to be developed and ready for successful implementation. These "tasks" and each "task" related information then can be recorded on the Program Development Control Chart, an example copy of which appears at the end of this section as Table 4.2.

The following questions, therefore, can be considered relevant in developing the program's human resources (other questions, of course, may also be relevant for a particular program):

Cell H1: How will the program's human resources become knowledgeable about the program's purpose and SMART goals?

Cell H2: In what particular ways do the program's human resources need to be informed or trained in how to make decisions using the program's eligibility standards and criteria?

Cell H3: In what ways do the program's human resources need to be knowledgeable about the program's policies and procedures?

Cell H4: Do the program's human resources require skills training in how to use particular methods and techniques?

Cell H5: Do the program's human resources require skills training in use of materials?

Cell H6: Skills training in use of the equipment?

Cell H7: (Typically not applicable.)

Cell H8: Do the program's human resources need to understand how the program is designed in terms of components, phases, and activities and how they relate to these elements?

Cell H9: Do the program's human resources need to be aware of budgetary parameters and procedures?

Cell H10: (Refers to the program's human resources.)

Cell H11: Have the incentives been considered that are relevant to maintain appropriate performance of the program's human resources?

Cell H12: How will the program's human resources be involved in the program evaluation plan and will they require training to become appropriately involved?

2.32 Develop the program's technological resources

This task involves use of the Technological Resource Dimension of the Program Development Matrix in relation to each element of the Program Design Elements Dimension of the Matrix. In this regard, various questions can help pinpoint the "technological resources program development tasks" that need to be accomplished in order for the human services program to be ready for successful implementation. These tasks and the related information then can be recorded on the Program Development Chart, an example copy of which appears at the end of this section as Table 4.2.

The following questions, therefore, can be considered relevant in developing the program's technological dimension (other questions, naturally, may also be relevant for a particular program).

Cell TE1: Have methods and procedures for measuring and evaluating goal attainment been decided?

Cell TE2: Have eligibility standards and criteria been determined?

Cell TE3: (Typically not applicable.)

Cell TE4: Have the exact methods and techniques been detailed?

Cell TE5: Have the materials been selected and ordered?

Cell TE6: Has equipment been selected and ordered?

Cell TE7: Have facilities been selected, built, upgraded, or changed as required?

Cell TE8: Can methods and techniques be used in the program's components as intended?

Cell TE9: (Typically not applicable.)

Cell TE10: (Typically not applicable.)

Cell TE11: (Typically not applicable.)

Cell TE12: Has program evaluation technology been determined?

2.33 Develop the program's informational resources

This task involves use of the Informational Resource Dimension of the Program Development Matrix in relation to each item of the Program Design Elements Dimension of the Matrix. Various questions, when answered, can lead to "informational resource

67

program development tasks" that can be recorded on the Program Development Control Chart (a copy can be found at the end of this section, seen as Table 4.2).

The following questions, therefore, can be considered relevant in developing the program's informational resources (other questions may also be relevant for a particular program):

Cell I1:   Is the program's purpose clear and are the program's goals SMART and documented?

Cell I2:   Are eligibility standards and criteria documented?

Cell I3:   Are policies and procedures documented?

Cell I4:   (Typically not applicable.)

Cell I5:   (Typically not applicable.)

Cell I6:   (Typically not applicable.)

Cell I7:   (Typically not applicable.)

Cell I8:   Are the program's components, phases, and activities documented?

Cell I9:   Is the program's budget approved?

Cell I10:   Are the program's personnel hired and known to all concerned?

Cell I11:   (Typically not applicable.)

Cell I12:   Has a program evaluation plan been documented?

2.34 Develop the program's financial resources

The following question can be considered the overarching one, and the most basically relevant one, with respect to *developing* the program's financial resources, using the Program Development Matrix and Program Development Control Chart:

Cell F9:   To what extent has a budget been delineated that seems to assure successful program implementation?

All other cells are typically not applicable.

2.35 Develop the program's physical resources

The following question can be considered the overarching one, and the most basically relevant one, with respect to developing the program's physical resources, using the Program Development Matrix (Table 4.1) and Program Development Control Chart (Table 4.2):

Cell P7: Have facilities been acquired, upgraded, and/or otherwise attended to, as a basis for successful program implementation?

All other cells are typically not applicable.

2.36 Develop the program's temporal resources

The following question can be considered the overarching one, and the most basically relevant one, with respect to developing the program's temporal resources, using the Program Development Matrix and Program Development Control Chart:

Cell TM8: To what extent is time allotted for the program's components, phases, and activities?

All other cells are typically not applicable.

Table 4.2: Program Development Control Chart

Task/Resource Dimension/Element	Personnel and Responsibilities	Indicators of Accomplishments	Timeframe	Comments

2.4 Document the Program Design

Through this program planning and evaluation activity, the design of the human services program is documented in written form, with respect to its essential elements. Basically, and most importantly, program design documentation is the culmination of appropriate completion of all other activities and tasks of the Design Phase. As a result, the program design document will include clear, concise, procedurally detailed, and cogent information about the following program design elements:

1. Purpose and SMART Goals.
2. Eligibility Standards and Criteria.
3. Policies and Procedures.
4. Methods and Techniques.

5. Materials.
6. Equipment.
7. Facilities.
8. Components, Phases, and Activities.
9. Budget.
10. Personnel.
11. Incentives.
12. Program Evaluation Plan.

The Program Design Review Worksheet, seen in Figure 4.2, can be used to make sure that all tasks and activities which have been discussed in this chapter have occurred.

Figure 4.2: Program Design Review Worksheet

Program Design Review Worksheet	
ELEMENT	**COMMENTS/RECOMMENDATIONS**
Target Population	
Needs of Target Population	
Relevant Context	
1. Purpose and Smart Goals	
2. Eligibility Standards and Criteria	
3. Policies and Procedures	
4. Methods and Techniques	
5. Materials	
6. Equipment	
7. Facilities	
8. Components, Phases, and Activities	
9. Budget	
10. Personnel	
11. Incentives	
12. Program Evaluation Plan	
Other	

chapter five

IMPLEMENTATION PHASE

In this section of the Resource Guide, the Implementation Phase is described in terms of its overarching purpose, constituent activities, technologies, and resulting products.

Purpose of the Implementation Phase

The Implementation Phase is the third of the four major phases of the program planning and evaluation process. The purpose of the Implementation Phase is to assure that the human services program that has been designed operates, over time, as expected, and that necessary modifications in how the program occurs are made by program implementers as well by other people who support program implementation, such as a program planning and evaluation team.

The Implementation Phase is very important for several reasons. These reasons include:

- When a human services program is designed via the program planning and evaluation process, the professional expectation is that the program will result in worthwhile outcomes for the participants (target population)—*if* the program is implemented according to design. Thus, precise ways to assure successful program implementation are necessary in order for these outcomes to be realized.

- Without making sure that a human services program is implemented as designed, the likelihood is decreased that worthwhile outcomes will result for the target population (participants).

- When it is clear as to actually what program is being implemented, there is a greater likelihood that more informed decisions will be made about what changes need to be made in the program, as it operates.

- Without documenting the program that actually has been implemented, it will not be possible to determine how the program contributed to outcomes, since the program will have been considered as a "black box" (unknown and nondocumentable).

Overview of the Activities of the Implementation Phase

Based on the above purpose and reasons, these are three major activities of the Implementation Phase. These activities are sequential, interrelated, and reflexive and they can be described as follows:

3.1 **Review the program design**, in order to make judgments about whether the program has been developed and whether it has been made ready for implementation.

3.2 **Facilitate program implementation**, whereby program implementers and other relevant stakeholders are involved purposely in the implementation process.

3.3 **Monitor program process**, in order to make judgments about whether the program is being implemented as designed and whether changes in the program are necessary.

The above three activities are *sequential* in that one activity must follow the other for a human services program to be implemented in a successful manner, according to its design. Further, these three activities are *interrelated* in that the information generated from one implementation activity serves to guide how to proceed with the next activity. Finally, the activities are *reflexive* in that changes in one activity and the resulting information from it may require re-routing of the program planning and evaluation team to a previously completed activity.

In the next section of this chapter, the first activity of the Implementation Phase – Review the Program Design – is discussed.

3.1 Review the Program Design

Through this program planning and evaluation activity, the design of the human services program which is to be implemented is reviewed by yourself, the client, and other relevant stakeholders. This review serves several important programmatic ends. These are:

- To assure that the design of the program still is relevant to the target population, their needs, and the relevant context. This focus is especially important when the program was designed at one point in time (e.g., spring months), but it is to be implemented at another point in time (e.g., fall months).

- To determine whether the program has been *developed* sufficiently, according to design, so that it can be implemented successfully.

- To consider other factors – human, technological, financial, organizational, etc. – that suggest implementation challenges, difficulties, or obstacles and how to respond to them.

In order to review the program design within the context of the Implementation Phase of the program planning and evaluation process, several tasks need to be accomplished by yourself with the client. These tasks are:

3.11 Specify and evaluate the elements of the program design.

3.12 Make necessary recommendations in preparation of the program design elements for successful program implementation.

3.13 Follow through on program design element recommendations.

3.14 Document a revised program design, as necessary.

Each of these tasks will be discussed below.

3.11 Specify and evaluate the elements of the program design

To specify the elements of the program design, it is necessary not only to have a framework for the program design elements but also a procedure for reviewing these elements. Relatedly, and most importantly, a program design document, and/or related information, that describes the program must be available in writing, in some form, to yourself and the client. Otherwise, this task cannot be accomplished successfully and the likelihood is decreased that the program will be implemented as designed.

The following are the relevant program elements (these are the same elements listed in Chapter Four).

1. **Purpose and SMART Goals** that can be considered as the basic reference point.

2. **Eligibility Standards and Criteria** that indicate what members of the target population can participate in the program.

3. **Policies and Procedures** that can guide program personnel in how to function within the program.

4. **Methods and Techniques** that are used by program personnel with participants as a means to facilitate goal attainment.

5. **Materials** that are used in conjunction with the methods and techniques.

6. **Equipment** that helps support program operations.

7. **Facilities** in which the program is implemented.

8. **Components, Phases, and Activities** that delineate that process of the program and how it will be implemented.

9. **Budget** that also supports program operators.

10. **Personnel** who are responsible for implementation of the program.

11. **Incentives** that help set the conditions so that program personnel and participants will want to follow through on the program.

12. **Program Evaluation Plan** that allows data to be gathered and analyzed so that judgments of worth or merit can be made about the program.

The procedure that can be used to make judgments about each of these program design elements involves use of a review document, such as the Program Design Evaluation Worksheet, a copy of which is seen in Figure 5.1.

Figure 5.1: Program Design Evaluation Worksheet

Program Design Element	Comments and Recommendations
1. Purpose and Smart Goals	
2. Eligibility Standards and Criteria	
3. Policies and Procedures	
4. Methods and Techniques	
5. Materials	
6. Equipment	
7. Facilities	
8. Components, Phases, and Activities	
9. Budget	
10. Personnel	
11. Incentives	
12. Program Evaluation Plan	

Using the worksheet, or another suitable form, each program design element is assessed as to three criteria. These are:

- **Clarity**—the extent to which the written information describing each particular element is understood by program implementers and others.

- **Compatibility**—the degree to which the element appears to be compatible and consistent with all other program design elements.

- **Development Status**—the extent to which the element appears sufficiently developed so as to be ready for successful implementation.

The judgments that are made by you and the client about the program design elements can be documented on the Program Design Evaluation Worksheet (see Figure 5.1). This documentation will serve as a basis for the task of making necessary recommendations in preparation of the program design elements, leading to successful program implementation. This task is discussed next.

3.12 Make necessary recommendations in preparation of the program design elements for successful program implementation

Once the elements of the program design have been specified and evaluated with relevant comments recorded on the Program Design Evaluation Worksheet (see Figure 5.1), it now is possible to collaborate with the client in making recommendations that appear necessary to support successful program implementation. In essence, the recommendations that are made can be considered as "final check points" before the program is implemented. These recommendations focus on preparation of the program for implementation, or "program implementation readiness." The recommendations are best addressed by placing them in a written list and by communicating them to all people who have a stake in the program's design, its implementation, and outcomes.

Although there may be any number of specific recommendations that can be made as part of this task, my research and professional experiences having to do with the process of program planning and evaluation for human services programs have indicated that recommendations are likely to be of the following kind:

1. **Purpose** statement needs to provide more specific answers as to the who, how, and what questions; program *goals* can be made "smarter" and communicated to people involved with the program.

2. **Eligibility standards and criteria** need to be made more explicit; alternatively, criteria may not be necessary for a program, as initially thought.

3. **Policies and procedures** need to be developed and communicated to the target population and program implementers.

4. **Methods and techniques** that are to be used in the program require more specificity or need refinement/customization, given the target population and their needs.

5. **Materials** for the program need to be procured.

6. **Equipment** for the program needs to be procured and tested.

7. **Facilities** need to be upgraded or improved according to explicit standards for health and safety.

8. **Components, phases, and activities** require additional specifications and linkage to one another in order to make the program internally consistent.

9. **Budget** requires additional specification and referencing to particular program design elements.

10. **Personnel** associated with the program can benefit from an orientation, education, and/or training.

11. **Incentives** that can facilitate successful implementation and follow through by program personnel need to be included in the design.

12. **Program evaluation plan** needs to be linked/become part of the program's design.

Once the recommendations have been made, the task now becomes that of following through on them. This task is discussed next.

3.13 Follow through on program design element recommendations

Naturally, if there are no program design element recommendations to be conveyed, then this task need not be accomplished. Typically, however, when the program design is reviewed, recommendations about design elements are the norm.

The task of following through on program design element recommendations can be accomplished in an effective and efficient way, if several conditions exist. These conditions can be referred to as the "3 Is". They are:

*   **Information**—It is made clear by the client or the person(s) responsible for program design and implementation, just *what* recommendations need to be acted upon, by *whom*, and *when* they need to be addressed and completed.

*   **Instrumentation**—The procedures, sanctions, authorizations, and supports (e.g., equipment) to act on the recommendations are available to the person(s) acting on them.

*   **Incentives**—There are sufficient incentives (intrinsic, extrinsic) for the person(s) acting on the recommendations to do so, including the formulation of candidates that foster sustained follow through.

When the "3 Is" are in place, there is a much greater likelihood that the program design element recommendations will be acted upon and followed through by those responsible for successful enactment. When they are not in place, you should not be surprised that the program is "less than ready" for successful implementation. Indeed, you might be able to predict a less than successful implementation effort at such a point in time.

3.14 Document a revised program design, as necessary

When the program is ready to be implemented, it is helpful to all concerned to make sure that these people understand what program is to be implemented. In that regard, it is recommended that the written program design document be revised to reflect the changes in the design elements. Without such revised documentation, too much is being left to change with respect to the understanding of people.

Once the program design document is revised and distributed to appropriate parties, attention can center on the second activity of the Implementation Phase – Facilitate Program Implementation. This second activity is discussed in the next section of the chapter.

3.2 Facilitate Program Implementation

Through this program planning and evaluation activity, the program that now is ready for implementation is given a "positive thrust" by means of program implementation facilitation. In this regard, facilitation of program implementation can be seen as a process, in and of itself, that consists of several sequential, interrelated activities (to be discussed below) that are intended to make implementation easier for all concerned. The activity of facilitation of program implementation is important for several reasons. These reasons include:

- A program, as reflected by its design, is essentially an abstraction until it begins to operate. However, there typically is an inert status about a program design that requires a stimulus for initiation.

- For a program to be implemented successfully, it usually must commence during certain "windows" of time and opportunity; otherwise, it may occur too late to be effective.

- The people involved with the program – target population, managers, staff, etc. - usually perceive a program more importantly, positively, and enthusiastically, when there is focused and thoughtful attention to implementation, especially when they are involved in the facilitation activity.

- Since considerable time, effort, and related expenditures have occurred relative to getting a program ready for implementation, it is desirable that these expenditures not go to waste due to a program that fails to be implemented.

In order to facilitate program implementation within the context of the Implementation Phase of the program planning and evaluation process, several tasks need to be accomplished by yourself with the client, other relevant stakeholders, and program implementers. These tasks can be organized by means of the acronym, DURABLE, which stand for the first letter of a series of implementation procedures, activities, and behaviors. These tasks are:

3.21 **D**iscuss the program with people who will be involved with and affected by its implementation.

3.22 **U**nderstand the needs and concerns of people with respect to implementation of the program.

3.23 **R**einforce people for appropriate involvement in program implementation.

3.24 **A**cquire the sanctions and supports that will contribute to successful program implementation.

3.25 **B**uild positive expectations of people about successful program implementation.

3.26 **L**earn to implement the program successfully, based on what is experienced as it occurs.

3.27 **E**valuate the process of program implementation in a planned, purposeful way.

Each of these tasks will be discussed below.

3.21 Discuss the program with people who will be involved with and affected by its implementation

By means of this task, it is possible for you, the client, and/or others involved with coordination and direction of the program to discuss it with a range of people. Essentially, these people may include the following types:

- Personnel who will be involved in the actual implementation and operation of the human services program (e.g., teachers, counselors, facilitators).

- Participants of the program (e.g., members of the target population which, typically, is often an overlooked group).

- Caregivers and significant others in the lives of program participants (e.g., parents/guardians, spouses, mentors).

- Professional administrators and other executives whose support is important to successful program implementation.

- Other relevant stakeholders such as representatives of community groups, funding agents, potential funders, the media, etc.

With respect to this task, *discussion* can be considered as any formal or informal activity aimed at: (a) informing people about the program's design and, (b) allowing people and opportunity to ask questions and comment about the program. In this regard, discussion activities are not to be construed solely in a narrow sense as trying to market the program as well as attract people to participate in it. Rather, discussion best occurs for all kinds of participants, and potential participants, including those target populations that are not voluntary groups but have been assigned to a program (e.g., elementary students for a reading program in a public school). In engaging people in discussion with respect to a human services program, the expectation is that this kind of program involvement is likely to not only increase their *awareness* of and *interest* in the program but also enhance their *desire* to support the program through purposeful and desirable *action*. Consequently, when worthwhile discussion occurs about the program, the likelihood is increased that it will be implemented more fully according to design, than without such discussion.

Although there is no one specific approach for engaging people in "human services program discussion", research and experience suggests the utility of use of the following guidelines (NB: These guidelines are applicable to any size program group, including an "n=1 program").

1. Prior to meeting with the particular people to discuss the program with them, send them a written notice about the discussion event. This notice should convey to each person the reason for this meeting, time frame, and what you would like to do at it (e.g., to hear their comments following a program design implementation). Naturally, the written message needs to be expressed in a language style appropriate to the group.

2. Arrange for a program discussion that occurs within a 15 to 30 minute time frame for the group, in a room or facility that can be considered comfortable and appropriate.

3. At the actual program discussion meeting, proceed according to the following kind of format:

    3.1 Welcome the group; thank them for their attendance.

    3.2 Encourage them to listen attentively and ask questions.

    3.3. Present and discuss the program according to the major program design elements, adapting the nature of discussion to the type of target group.

    3.4 Answer all questions and indicate how non-answered questions will be responded to (e.g., follow up meeting, phone call) subsequent to the discussion.

    3.5 Specify how and to whom people can further discuss the program, when it is implemented.

4. Follow up with the group, or individuals therein, if they have made any specific requests for information, or if you need to provide additional information to them.

As a result of the program discussion, the people affected by the program and who are involved with its implementation should have participated in a positive educational experience and they should have been involved in worthwhile and appropriate social interaction.

3.22 Understand the needs and concerns of people with respect to implementation of the program

Through this task, you, the client, and others seek to *understand* (become knowledgeable about) how different people who are involved or otherwise affected by the human services program view it. Understanding of such needs and concerns of individuals and groups is important for several reasons:

- A program is like any other entity: it can be perceived differently by individuals, depending on a number of factors including their own understanding of it, values, etc.

- If the perceptions and understanding that a person has about a human services program are similar to those reflected by the program's design, the likelihood is increased that their involvement in the program's operation will be aligned with their expected roles and responsibilities.

- When a person's perceptions and understanding about a program are different then what is expected, such differences are best addressed prior to implementation.

"Understanding activities" can occur through both formal and informal means. With respect to a formal approach, it is helpful to ask people about their understanding of the human services program, following discussion of it with them. Toward, this end, individuals (e.g., implementers, participants, others) can be asked via a survey instrument or other such form to provide their responses to the following questions (in their own words and language style, of course):

1. What are the purpose and goals of the program?
2. Why is the program important? To what individuals and groups?
3. What does the program consist of?
4. When ready, will the program be able to operate?

From answers to these questions, you will have obtained information from program implementers, participants, and/or others about their understanding of important aspects of the program's design. Then, based on this information, you will be able to decide what kinds of actions need to be taken to enhance program understanding or, depending on the nature and scope of their responses, you can initiate program design changes.

The above kinds of questions, of course, also can be asked of individuals in an informal, less systematic way. However, the responses should be considered the same as with a more formal approach. Moreover, and most importantly, "program understanding activities" can occur not only prior to program implementation but throughout the program implementation process. In this way, you, the client, and others are able to keep up to date about people, their needs, and concerns relative to the program as it proceeds, over time.

3.23 Reinforce people for appropriate involvement in program implementation

The program *reinforcement* task is intended to set the "psychological conditions" so that people who are involved in program implementation will want to perform in a quality way. Naturally, however, for people to want to perform well in a program implementation sense, their 3Rs – **R**oles, **R**esponsibilities, and **R**elationships – need to be understood by them. If a program design has been formulated that is clear, compatible, and developmentally sound, program personnel will have a sound understanding of their 3Rs with respect to the human services program. If such a program design has not been formulated, then these people's understanding must be addressed in a way that they become particularly informed about their 3Rs.

Reinforcement of personnel for appropriate implementation of a human services program can occur in a meaningful way through utilization of the following guidelines by the client, yourself, and the person responsible for the direction of the program:

1. For each person (program implementer), make sure that they are informed about their program 3Rs (roles, responsibilities, relationships) in clear written form.

2. Provide an opportunity for each program implementer to be able to discuss their program 3Rs, with their program supervisor, in order to clarify program implementation parameters, etc.

3. Monitor the extent to which the program implementer is following through on their program 3Rs by means of onsite observations, meetings, and relevant reviews of permanent products.

4. Provide positive social reinforcement when presenting program personnel with feedback about their performance (informal continuous; formal periodic).

5. Provide public recognition to implementers for sound and outstanding performance, based on their program 3Rs.

6. Make all monetary (if possible) and non-monetary incentives contingent on appropriate display of program 3Rs by the implementers. Do so in a timely, reliable, and valid way.

By means of the above guidelines as well as through routine interactions and feedback with program implementers, it is likely that they will want to follow through on their program 3Rs in quality ways. Resultantly, they are more likely to be satisfied with their work and desirous of continuing with it.

3.24 Acquire the sanctions and supports that will contribute to successful program implementation

For a human services program to be implemented successfully, it often is the case that particular sanctions and supports need to be in place – *acquired* – prior to program implementation. In this regard, *sanctions* have to do with such entities as authorizations, endorsements, or agreements from individuals and groups who have authority or some major responsibility for a human services program. Relatedly, *supports* reflect particular resources that will help assure successful program implementation.

Sanctions and supports that need to be acquired are usefully considered with respect to the elements of the program's design. When sanctions and supports are referenced to the program design, it then is possible to consider to what extent some combination of the following require acquisition:

Sanctions
- Endorsement from the chief administrator or executive that the program is *targeted* to important needs of a particular *population.*
- Statements from key officials and stakeholders that the *purpose* and *goals* of the program are valuable and worthwhile.
- Statements about the relevance of the program's *eligibility standards and criteria.*
- Concurrence with program coordinators and personnel that the program's *policies* and *procedures* are necessary, relevant, and that appropriate consequences will be applied contingent to them.

Supports
- Time to train program implementers in correct application of the *methods* and *techniques* to be used in the program.
- Assistance in procuring *materials* and *equipment* for the program.
- Qualified people to upgrade and maintain *facilities.*
- Training programs to assure that program *personnel* can follow through on the program's *components, phases* and *activities.*
- Adequate *budget* that will contribute to program operations.
- Understanding and appreciation of the importance of *incentives* for personnel and participants of the program.

Although a program design-focused approach to acquisition of sanctions and supports may seem to some people as too constraining, in practice the range of sanctions and supports that are relevant are readily identified and addressed as part of the process of program implementation.

3.25 Build positive expectations of people about successful program implementation

This task focuses on a very important, albeit overlooked, challenge: Implementation of a program in a way that adds value to be particular target population. Clearly, human services programs are not implemented in a mechanistic, pedantic manner. The realities that such programs are implemented with "real people" in "real time settings", where the environment cannot be treated as error variance, creates a situation where people will be skeptical about whether the program will be effective. In particular, the likelihood certainly exists that program personnel may be less than certain and confident that the program can have positive impacts.

When you, the client, and other key stakeholders make sure that personnel are supported in terms of positive beliefs and expectations for successful program implementation and outcome, a valuable program implementation will have resulted for them. In this regard, it is recommended that positive *beliefs* and *confidence* be manifested about such matters as the following:

- *Purpose* and *goals* of the program are worthy, especially in relation to the *needs* of the *target population.*

- Potential effectiveness of the *methods and techniques* used in the program.

- Responsiveness of the program participants to the *materials, equipment,* and *facilities.*

- Other matters, specific to each program.

3.26 Learn to implement the program based on what is experienced as it occurs

The implementation of a human services program can be considered as a process in and of itself. Within the context of this program implementation process, a challenge for program personnel and their supervisors is a continuous one: Learn how to implement the program in the best way possible, once it is in operation. This task of the DURABLE approach focuses on helping to assure that "program implementation learning" occurs in a systematic, ongoing way.

Although the quantity and quality of such learning that is needed for program personnel will vary depending upon the nature and scope of the program and relevant contextual factors, it is important to determine what may need to be learned, why, and when. Toward that end, Figure 5.1 on page 74 provides a visual framework that can be used for that purpose by yourself, the client, and other people concerned with successful program implementation. As seen in Figure 5.1 on page 74 the vertical dimension delineates the elements of the program's design that are to be implemented. In juxtaposition, the horizontal dimension of Figure 5.1 allows for the description of three separate yet interrelated dimensions that can be applied to each program implementer relative to each program design element. These *KSA* dimensions are **K**nowledge that program implementers need to acquire for continued implementation; **S**kills of a technical nature that may need to be developed as the program operates; and **A**bilities (e.g., time management) that program implementers may need to use effectively within the program process.

3.27 Evaluating the process of program implementation in a planned, purposeful way

This task is addressed and discussed next as the next major activity (3.3) of Implementation Phase – Monitor Program Process.

3.3 Monitor Program Process

Through this program planning and evaluation activity, judgments are made by yourself, the client and other relevant stakeholders, including program implementers, about the extent to which the human services program has been implemented according to its design. In this regard, the focus of all concerned is on the *process* of the implementation of the program, particularly *variations in the process* and what those variations are likely to mean for a resulting, worthwhile program (e.g., whether goals are attained; extent to which value is added to program participants).

The monitoring of the process of a human services program is important for several reasons. These reasons include:

- A program is expected to proceed according to its design, based on the assumption that if it does so, then worthwhile outcomes will result. In order to facilitate such a likelihood, the process of program implementation needs to be monitored.

- In order to make judgments about whether the program has been implemented, process control limits of variation need to be established and evaluated. Otherwise, it will not be known whether the program is proceeding in desired ways.

- As a program is implemented, the possibility always exists that revisions in elements of the program's design may need to occur. In making decisions about program revision, a basic point of reference is the process the program was intended to take and how revisions are likely to alter the program implementation process.

- To document exactly what program has been implemented as a basis for program reporting purposes that is to be used in program evaluation.

In order to *monitor* the *process* of the *implementation* of a human services program, it first and foremost is crucial to understand the program's design. With such an understanding, it then is possible to decide how each of the program's design elements is to be implemented and how such implementation can be considered from a process control perspective. Naturally, if the design of a human services program is not documented and understood, the activity of monitoring program process will be a fruitless, frustrating one. Thus, it comes as no surprise that the activity of monitoring program process can best occur only by following through on a set of separate, yet interrelated, tasks. These tasks, which relate in large part to the program's design elements, are the following (the respective program design elements are noted in parenthesis):

3.31   Determine what people, with what needs, have been participating in the program (Target Population; Needs).

3.32 Decide whether the program's purpose and goals are being addressed (Purpose and SMART Goals).

3.33 Judge whether the program's eligibility standards and criteria are being utilized (Eligibility Standards and Criteria).

3.34 Determine whether policies and procedures of the program are being followed (Policies and Procedures).

3.35 Assess whether methods, techniques, materials, equipment, and facilities are being used as anticipated (Methods and Techniques; Materials; Equipment; Facilities).

3.36 Judge the extent to which the components, phases and activities of the program are occurring as planned (Components, Phases, and Activities).

3.37 Consider whether the budget is being expended as authorized (Budget).

3.38 Identify how program personnel are performing their roles and responsibilities (Personnel).

3.39 Decide whether incentives are being applied within the program as intended (Incentives).

3.310 Determine whether program evaluation activities are occurring as planned (Program Evaluation Plan).

Key Notions and Terms

Each of the above tasks will be discussed in the remainder of this chapter of the book with respect to the notions of program process control, process control limits and process control limit indicators (upper and lower), as well as in terms of methods of program process monitoring. More particularly, *program process control* refers to the painstaking precise, but enjoyable, challenge of making sure that the human services program is proceeding (being implemented), according to the way it was designed. Relatedly, the term, *process control limits*, refers to the extent to which a program may vary according to its design, beyond particular limits; *process control limit indicators* are benchmarks that allow you, the client, and other relevant stakeholders to make judgments about whether, and to what extent, the process of the program exceeds process control limits. *Program process monitoring methods* are the procedures, techniques, and/or instruments for gathering data on the process of the implementation of the human services program.

As you review the information for each of the tasks that follow, please note that the examples used are provided in a generic sense and, as such, are *not* referenced to the implementation of any particular human services program. Such referencing, naturally, must occur only with respect to a particular program design, within a particular context.

3.31 Determine what people, with what needs, have been participating in the program (Target Population; Needs)

Process Control Limit Indicators

Upper Control Limit (UCL)	People are being included in the program who do not possess needs and characteristics of the target population.
Expected Control Limit (ECL)	Program participants with needs and characteristics of the target population are participating in the program.
Lower Control Limit (LCL)	People are being excluded from the program who possess needs and characteristics of the target population.

Program Process Monitoring Methods

1. Review of program registration records.
2. Descriptive reports provided by program coordinator or implementers.

3.32 Decide whether the program's purpose and goals are being addressed (Purpose and SMART Goals)

Process Control Limit Indicators

Upper Control Limit (UCL)	The program's purpose and goals are not being addressed, but other goals not included in the program's design are being addressed.
Expected Control Limit (ECL)	The program's purpose and goals are being addressed in terms of the program's technology.
Lower Control Limit (LCL)	Some aspect of the program's purpose and/or some goals are being addressed in too narrow or constricted a way.

Program Process Monitoring Methods

1. Review the program reports, lesson plans, and session plans.
2. Interviews and planned discussions with program implementers.

3.33 Judge whether the program's eligibility standards and criteria are being utilized (Eligibility Standards and Criteria)

Process Control Limit Indicators

Upper Control Limit (UCL)	The program's eligibility standards and criteria are being used too loosely or not at all, thereby including ineligible people.
Expected Control Limit (ECL)	The program's eligibility standards and criteria are being used in a way that conforms to the program's design.
Lower Control Limit (LCL)	The program's eligibility standards and criteria are being used too restrictively, thereby excluding eligible participants.

Program Process Monitoring Methods

1. Statistical comparisons of program participants with non-program participants in relation to the eligibility standards and criteria as "discriminants".
2. Review of program records describing participants.

3.34 Determine whether policies and procedures of the program are being followed (Policies and Procedures)

Process Control Limit Indicators

Upper Control Limit (UCL)	The program's policies and procedures are being followed too loosely or not at all.
Expected Control Limit (ECL)	The program's policies and procedures are being followed according to program design.
Lower Control Limit (LCL)	The program's policies and procedures are being followed too restrictively.

Program Process Monitoring Methods

1. Review of critical incidents reported about policy and procedural variations.
2. Planned interviews and discussions with program implementers.

3.35 Assess whether methods, techniques, materials, equipment, and facilities are being used as anticipated (Methods and Techniques; Materials; Equipment; Facilities)

Process Control Limit Indicators

Upper Control Limit (UCL)   The program's methods, techniques, materials, equipment, and facilities are being used too loosely or not at all.

Expected Control Limit (ECL)   The program's methods, techniques, materials, equipment, and facilities are being used as anticipated.

Lower Control Limit (LCL)   The program's methods, techniques, materials, equipment, and facilities are being used restrictively.

Program Process Monitoring Methods

1. Review of program records and reports.
2. Comments from the program implementers.
3. Direct observation of the program's implementation.

3.36 Judge the extent to which the components, phases, and activities of the program are occurring as planned (Components, Phases, and Activities)

Process Control Limit Indicators

Upper Control Limit (UCL)   The program's components, phases, and activities are occurring too loosely; other components, phases, and activities not part of the program's design are occurring.

Expected Control Limit (ECL)   The program's components, phases, and activities are occurring according to the design.

Lower Control Limit (LCL)   The program's components, phases, and activities are occurring too restrictively; some components, phases, and activities are not occurring.

Program Process Monitoring Methods

1. Review the program records and reports.
2. Comments for the program implementers.
3. Direct observation of the program's implementation.

3.37 Consider whether the budget is being expended as authorized

Process Control Limit Indicators

Upper Control Limit (UCL)	The program's budget is being expended on items not authorized for it, as part of the program's design.
Expected Control Limit (ECL)	The program's budget is being expended as authorized.
Lower Control Limit (LCL)	The program's budget is being expended too restrictively; necessary items are not being funded, although authorization for those items has been approved.

Program Process Monitoring Methods

1. Review the program records including budget expenditures.
2. Comments from program implementers.

3.38 Identify how program personnel are performing their roles and responsibilities

Process Control Limit Indicators

Upper Control Limit (UCL)	Program personnel are performing roles and responsibilities not included as part of the program's design.
Expected Control Limit (ECL)	Program personnel are performing their roles and responsibilities according to the program's design.
Lower Control Limit (LCL)	Program personnel are performing their roles and responsibilities in too restrictive a manner; some are not being performed.

Program Process Monitoring Methods

1. Planned interviews with program coordinator or director.
2. Observation of program operations.

3.39 Decide whether incentives are being applied with the program as intended

Process Control Limit Indicators

Upper Control Limit (UCL)   Incentives are not being applied appropriately.

Expected Control Limit (ECL)   Incentives are being applied as intended.

Lower Control Limit (LCL)   Incentives are not being applied at all.

Program Process Monitoring Methods

1. Planned interviews with program coordinator or director.
2. Planned interviews with program implementers.
3. Reviews of relevant program records.

3.310 Determine whether program evaluation activities are occurring as planned

Process Control Limit Indicators

Upper Control Limit (UCL)   Program evaluation activities are occurring in ways that exceed or otherwise deviate from the program evaluation plan.

Expected Control Limit (ECL)   Program evaluation activities are occurring as planned.

Lower Control Limit (LCL)   Program evaluation activities are not occurring at all.

Program Process Monitoring Methods

1. Planned interviews with program coordinator or director.
2. Reviews of relevant program records.

The next chapter deals with the Evaluation Phase of the program planning and evaluation process, which is the final phase of the program planning and evaluation process.

chapter six

EVALUATION PHASE

In this section of the Resource Guide, the Evaluation Phase of the program planning and evaluation process is described in terms of its overarching purpose, constituent activities, technologies, and resulting products.

Purpose of the Evaluation Phase

The Evaluation Phase is the fourth of the four major phases of the program planning and evaluation process. The purpose of the Evaluation Phase is to assure that data are gathered and analyzed with respect to important program evaluation questions, with the resulting evaluation information enabling sound judgments to be made about the worth (value) of the program, thereby contributing to continuous program development and improvement.

With respect to the program planning and evaluation process, the Evaluation Phase actually begins during the Design Phase when a program evaluation plan is formulated and included as one of the design elements of the human services program. Unfortunately, however, there are many human services programs where a program evaluation plan has not been included as part of the design of the program. In fact, in many of these instances, the program's design itself is not clear! Thus, in programmatic situations where a program's design is not clear and/or when there is no program evaluation plan "built into" the program, the Evaluation Phase as described in this chapter can serve as a springboard for sound program evaluation and, hence, lead to program planning.

The Evaluation Phase is very important for a range of reasons. These reasons vary from more intrinsic professional needs to extrinsic bureaucratic concerns. These reasons are:

- A human services program is an investment of resources. These resources include human, technological, informational, financial, temporal, and physical resources. For professionals associated with delivery of human services, it is expected that focused concerns exist to assure that the program (investment) adds value to the target population (in terms of addressing particular psychological and educational needs). Such assurances of this nature can only occur by means of sound program evaluation (the notion of sound program evaluation will be discussed below).

- A human services program exists in psychological space and physical location, and it proceeds over time in a way that is anticipated as being in accord with its program design. As a human services program is designed and implemented, therefore, the professional task becomes one of making sure that the program is continually improved, based on the value it has for the target population. Continuous program development and improvement, therefore, can be facilitated by sound program evaluation.

- If a human services program does add value to a target population, the issue then can be raised as to whether the program should be continued and even expanded to other sites and target groups, relative to the investment as reflected by the program's design. If it is determined that the program has limited or no value, it likely should be eliminated or adjusted in some way. However, in order for such program planning decisions to be made, evaluation information about the program's value and how it has been implemented must be obtained and placed into an understandable form.

- A human services program may need to be understood and/or otherwise reviewed by individuals, groups, and organizations that fund the program. These "external entities" may be ones such as boards of education, state departments, federal agencies, or private foundations. A sound program evaluation that addresses specific external concerns can help assure continuation of program funds and operation.

- A sound program evaluation that is reflected as an important element of the design of the program is likely to be a means for involving program implementers and other key stakeholders in matters of continuous program improvement and related value added concerns.

Qualities of a Sound Human Services Program Evaluation

As part of both the Design Phase and the Evaluation Phase, how program evaluation will proceed with respect to a human services program will be reflected in a program evaluation plan. In this regard, a sound program evaluation plan (to be discussed below) enhances the likelihood that a sound evaluation of the human services program will occur. As such, a sound program evaluation is one that possesses the following qualities:

- **Practical**   the program evaluation plan can be implemented by people in the organization in a way that is not disruptive to organizational routines (e.g., the process of teaching and learning; a manufacturing production process).

- **Useful**   the information that is generated as a result of the program evaluation plan allows the client and other relevant stakeholders to make more informed decisions about the program and how to improve it.

- **Proper**   the program evaluation occurs in ways that adhere to all relevant ethical standards and legal requirements that are pertinent to the program.

- **Technically Defensible**   the program evaluation plan includes methods, procedures, and instruments that can be justified as to their reliability, validity, and accurateness, given the program evaluation questions (to be discussed below).

Overview of the Activities of the Evaluation Phase

Based on the above purpose and reasons, there are twelve major activities of the Evaluation Phase as part of the program planning and evaluation process. These activities are sequential, interrelated, and reflexive. They can be described, in overview form, as follows:

4.1   **Identify the client** (or client group) that has expressed concern, in some way, about development and improvement of a human services program (NB: if you are a coordinator or director of such a program, you may well be "your own client")

4.2   **Determine the client's needs for program evaluation** that may not even be readily apparent to you or the client but that may reflect extrinsic matters (e.g., need to comply with a board directive) or more intrinsic matters (e.g., desire to improve the lives of people).

4.3   **Place the program to be evaluated into "evaluable" form**, by describing the design of the program according to its important design elements so that it will be clear to all concerned as to what actually is being evaluated.

4.4   **Delineate program evaluation questions** that, if answered appropriately, will inform the client and other relevant stakeholders about the program's value and how to proceed to develop and improve the program.

4.5   **For each program evaluation question, specify the data collection variables** that will allow data to be collected in order to answer the question.

4.6   **Describe the data collection methods, instruments, and procedures** that will allow data to be collected on the data collection variables in order to answer each program evaluation question.

4.7   **Describe the methods and procedures for data analysis** that will be used to make sense of the data that have been collected in response to each program evaluation question.

4.8   **Specify program evaluation personnel and responsibilities**, so that the program evaluation can occur as planned.

4.9 **Delineate guidelines for communication and use of program evaluation information**, for each program evaluation question, so that a sound program evaluation will occur and serve as a basis for program planning.

4.10 **Construct program evaluation protocols**, by placing the information generated about how to answer each program evaluation question into a coherent, written form (based on information from steps 1-9 above).

4.11 **Implement the program evaluation**, as delineated in the program evaluation plan, making necessary changes in the plan as the evaluation proceeds.

4.12 **Evaluate the program evaluation**, with respect to its soundness (practicality, utility, propriety, technical defensibility).

Before these program evaluation activities are described in a step by step way, some key terms need to be considered.

Key Terms

In order to effectively collaborate and communicate with your client, program implementers, and other relevant stakeholders as part of the Evaluation Phase, there are several terms that are important to understand. These terms are:

- **Program Evaluation** — the process of making judgments about the worth or merit (value) of a human services program (as reflected by the Evaluation Phase of the program planning and evaluation process).

- **Program Evaluation Plan** — includes all the program evaluation protocols that will allow data to be gathered and analyzed with respect to the program evaluation questions. Relatedly, and most importantly, the program evaluation plan is an important element of a human services program design.

- **Program Evaluation Protocol** — a written document that specifies how each program evaluation question will be answered. The protocol details the following:
  - The program evaluation question;
  - Data collection variables;
  - Data collection methods, instruments, procedures;
  - Methods and procedures for data analysis;
  - Guidelines for communication and use of evaluation information.

Now, each program evaluation activity will be considered, in more depth, in the reminder of this chapter.

4.1 Identify the Client

Through this program planning and evaluation activity, the client for the evaluation of the program is identified. In this regard, the client may well be the same individual and/or group who has been the client through the entire program planning and evaluation process, to date. On some occasions, however, especially when external funding agents or agencies are stakeholders in the program, people associated with such entities may need to be identified as a client. On other occasions, however, it is possible that you may be own client, especially if you are the person responsible for direction or coordination of the human services program.

Client identification for program evaluation purposes can be guided by asking and answering the following questions:

- Who is the individual or group within the human services organization that is directly responsible for assuring that the program is implemented as designed?

- Who is the individual or group within the human services organization that is responsible for overseeing the program, while also functioning in a larger managerial or administrative capacity?

- Who is the individual, group, or agency that is external to the human services organization that is interested in the design, implementation, and outcomes of the program?

By asking and answering these questions, you will determine whether you have one client, or multiple clients, for program evaluation purposes. In this regard, you then will be in a clearer position to identify your primary client and place any other clients into appropriate perspectives and time frames.

4.2 Determine the Clients' Needs for Program Evaluation

Through this program evaluation activity, the reasons for a program evaluation are discussed with the client and a determination is made about the nature and scope of the client's program evaluation needs. Then, a subsequent decision is made about whether those needs can be addressed by means of program evaluation. Determination of the client's program evaluation needs is important for several reasons. These reasons are:

- When a client has clarified their understanding of why a program evaluation is needed, the likelihood is increased that they will be involved in an effective way in seeing to it that the program evaluation is planned appropriately and that it occurs as planned.

- When the needs that a client has for program evaluation are made explicit, you are in a sound position for deciding whether and to what extent those needs can be addressed by means of program evaluation.

- When the needs of a client with respect to program evaluation have been determined, it is possible to assess the client's current understanding of and expectations for the program planning and evaluation process.

In order to determine the needs of the client for program evaluation, several tasks should be accomplished by yourself with the client. These tasks are:

4.21   Specify what the client wants to know or learn about the program.
4.22   Pinpoint why the client wants this knowledge.
4.23   Assess how the client expects this knowledge to be acquired.

Each of these tasks will be discussed below.

4.21 Specify what the client wants to know or learn about

It is important to specify what the client wants to know or learn about the program. With this information, it then becomes possible to identify what aspect of the program's design is of concern to the client. In this regard, you can ask the client to answer the following questions:

- I (client) would like to know about _____ with respect to the program?
- I (client) would like to know the following things about the program: _____ _____?

The answers of the client to this request can then be categorized by you as client program evaluation needs as follows:

	Current	**Desired**
WHO	Client lacks knowledge as to whether the program has addressed the appropriate target population.	Client has knowledge as to whether the program has addressed the appropriate target population.
	Current	**Desired**
HOW	Client does not know whether and to what extent the program has been *implemented* according to design.	Client knows whether and to what extent the program has been *implemented* according to design.
	Current	**Desired**
WHAT	Client does not know whether and to what extent the program has *added value* to the target population.	Client knows whether and to what extent the program has *added value* to the target population.

As a result of specifying what the client wants to know or learn, in a "needs structure sense," the client then can be more specifically assisted, via program evaluation, to become a more knowledgeable stakeholder.

4.22 Pinpoint why the client wants this knowledge

Once it is understood what knowledge the client wants to possess about the human services program, it is helpful to assist the client to make sure that the resulting evaluation information will really be perceived as helpful to that individual. Toward that end, the client can be assisted in "thinking through" why they really want to be increasingly informed about the program. This task can be accomplished by asking the client to answer the following questions:

- Why do I want to know _____ about the program?

- If I learned _____ about the program, what would that knowledge do for me with respect to the program's continuous development or improvement?

The response of the client to this request can then be considered by you in making judgments about whether the client can be assisted, via program evaluation, at the present time and/or at some time in the near future.

4.23 Assess how the client expects this program knowledge to be acquired

In planning for a program evaluation, it is helpful to understand how the client perceives the Evaluation Phase, or the program evaluation process. Some clients will have had prior experience with program evaluation. For these clients, they may realize that the evaluation of a program is not a unitary event but, rather a systemic process. In contrast, some clients will not have previously been involved in program evaluation. For these clients, expectations about what might be accomplished as part of a program evaluation may be unrealistic or they may have a narrow version of program evaluation (e.g. a program evaluation is synonymous with an evaluation instrument or with a research project). Whatever the situation, assessing how a client expects program evaluation information to be obtained will assist you in working with the client toward a sound program evaluation.

4.3 Place the Program to be Evaluated into the "Evaluable" Form

Through this program planning and evaluation activity, the human services program that is going to be evaluated is placed into a form where sound evaluation can occur. Within the context of the planning and evaluation process, this product is referred to as an "evaluable program". An evaluable program is one that reflects a program design that meets three criteria (you may recall that these criteria were initially mentioned in the Design Phase chapter):

- **Clarity**—the extent to which written information describing each program design element exists and the degree to which the design of the program is understood by yourself, the client, and other relevant stakeholders.

- **Compatibility**—the degree to which each program design element appears to be compatible/consistent with all other elements.

- **Development status**—the extent to which each program design element appears sufficiently developed so as to be ready for successful implementation; or, if the program is implemented, how developed is the program in terms of its resources.

Placing the program to be evaluated into an evaluable form (i.e., a program design that is clear and compatible with its development status understood) is important to you, the client and other relevant stakeholders for several reasons.

These reasons include:

- Through the planning and evaluation process, a major, indeed most fundamental task is continuous development and improvement of a human services *program* that adds value to people (target population). This task cannot be successfully completed, however, unless the program is clearly understood by all concerned as to its essential design elements.

- In order to develop and improve a program, outcomes of the program are considered not as "isolated entities" but rather in relation to the *program* that was implemented, the program that was intended to be implemented, *and* the target population, prior to and during the time that the program was in operation. To make such judgments, though, the program's design needs to be evaluable.

- In many instances, a human services program is considered by the client and others (e.g. agency administrators) as a candidate for implementation in one or more other settings. Thus, exactly what program is the candidate for implementation in other sites must be understood by all concerned.

- The task of designing a program, including its development, involves a range of resources (e.g. people, time, technology). Given these resource energy expenditures, and the concern for adding value to people through a program, knowing just what program is expected to "bring in the return" is sound professional practice, as a basis for evaluation.

Naturally, if you have been following the program planning and evaluation process described in the chapters of this book, you will already have proceeded through at least the Clarification Phase and Design Phase. If you followed through on the activities and tasks of these phases, according to the guidelines presented in those chapters, an evaluable program design will have resulted through your efforts, the client, the program planning and evaluation team, and any other relevant stakeholders.

If you are involved with a client in evaluating a program that, heretofore, has not been placed into evaluable program design form, you have the task of generating such a written product with the client and others. You can involve the client toward that end by using the activities of the Design Phase. Otherwise, without doing so, the likelihood is diminished greatly that a sound program evaluation can occur and the opportunity will be wasted for productively involving people in continuous development and improvement of a human services program.

4.4 Delineate Program Evaluation Questions

Through this program planning and evaluation activity, the program evaluation questions on which an evaluation will focus are delineated and agreed upon by the client and other relevant stakeholders, in conjunction with yourself as the consultant. In this regard, a *program evaluation question* can be considered to be a question about some element of the program's design, its implementation, or results that, if answered, will allow particular program planning and evaluation actions to be taken by yourself, the client, and other relevant stakeholders. These possible actions include:

- Judgments about the worth (merit, value) of the program in serving the needs of the target population

- Judgment about the worth of the program in adding value to people

- Judgments about the capability of the program to be implemented or designed

- Judgments about the program in terms of its contribution to the organization

- Decisions about how to use the evaluation information resulting from the evaluation to make revisions in the program's design

- Decisions about whether and to what extent the program can be implemented in other settings

- Decisions about whether elements of the program's design should be eliminated or whether the entire program should be terminated/phased out

Although all of these actions will not typically be taken as part of a particular program evaluation, the utility of any program evaluation question being asked and answered rests with the extent to which the answer to the question (evaluation information) will facilitate at least one of the aforementioned actions.

In order to delineate program evaluation questions that will facilitate effective and efficient program planning and evaluation actions, therefore, there are several tasks that can be accomplished by yourself, in conjunction with the client and others. These tasks are:

4.41 Specify what needs to be known about the program, as a basis for effective and efficient program planning and evaluations actions.

4.42 Generate an initial list of program evaluation questions.

4.43 Select the most important questions to be answered, placing them into SMART program evaluation form.

Although each of these tasks will be discussed below, it can be noted here that when you finalize each program evaluation question, you can initiate a Program Evaluation Protocol Worksheet for that question. This can be initiated by placing each question at the top of a worksheet, along with the title of the program, client identification information, and the date. A copy of the Program Evaluation Protocol Worksheet is seen as Figure 6.1.

Figure 6.1: Program Evaluation Protocol Worksheet

PROGRAM EVALUATION PROTOCOL WORKSHEET	
Program:	Client
Date:	Program Evaluation Question No.
DATA COLLECTION VARIABLES	
DATA COLLECTION METHODS, INSTRUMENTS, PROCEDURES (attach relevant instrumentation to this protocol)	
METHODS AND PROCEDURES FOR DATA ANALYSIS	
PROGRAM EVALUATION PERSONNEL AND RESPONSIBILITIES	
GUIDELINES FOR COMMUNICATION AND USE OF PROGRAM EVALUATION INFORMATION	

4.41 Specify what needs to be known about the program, as a basis for effective program planning and evaluation actions

By successfully completing this task, you will be able to know what actions the client would like to take that relate to the program planning and evaluation and why the client would like to take such actions. Typically, you will have to guide the client and others (e.g. program planning and evaluation team) toward these ends, unless they are experienced in program planning and evaluation.

There are several steps that you can take with the client and others to address the above matters:

1. You can rely on the knowledge that you already have on what the client needs to/ wants to know about the program, based on the tasks already completed (see Tasks 4.21 – 4.23).

2. You can use the existing knowledge that you have about the client's program evaluation information needs to discuss with them the particular planning and evaluation actions that can be taken through obtaining this information. In this regard, you can decide with the client whether by "learning what they want to know" about the program and, via the program evaluation information to be generated, it will help them in facilitating effective and efficient program planning and evaluation actions such as:

    • Being able to make precise and evaluative judgments about whether and to what extent the needs of the target population have been addressed.

    • Being able to make confident statements that the program was worthwhile in that it appears to have been a contributing factor in adding value to the target population.

    • Being able to draw reasonable conclusions that the program was implemented as designed, or that it was changed in some way.

    • Being able to make judgments that the program may be valuable enough to continue to implement it in the organization and/or to expand to other sites.

    • Decisions about making revisions in program design elements such as in the following:

        i.   Purpose and goals
        ii.   Sequence and timing of activities
        iii. Methods and material
        iv.   Personnel and their responsibilities
        v.   Other design elements

At this point, the important thing is to seek to make sure that a client's "need to know" about a program can be related to a particular program evaluation question, and that the answer to each question will facilitate an effective and efficient program planning and evaluation action.

4.42 Generate an initial list of program evaluation questions

By successfully completing this task, you will have generated an initial list of program evaluation questions. Then, once you have come up with a list, the most important of these questions then can be selected, eventually being placed into "SMART program evaluation form".

Although there are various ways that an initial list of program evaluation questions may be generated by yourself, with the client and other relevant stakeholders, the following brainstorming method has been found to be a practical and meaningful one:

1. Have each individual (e.g. client, team members) separately list on a separate sheet of paper, what they (each one) consider to be important program evaluation questions (after you give them a definition of a program evaluation question).

2. Ask each individual to state one of their questions and why they consider it important. You can place it on a white board or a flip chart.

3. Proceed in this manner until all questions (and reasons why) have been presented and listed.

4. Discussion can ensue with the individual/group about similarities and differences between and among questions and comments made about other questions not so listed that seem to encompass two or more listed ones.

5. An edited and *initial* set of program evaluation questions is agreed upon.

There are virtually an endless number of program evaluation questions that can be generated about human services programs. However, no matter what the possible amount, they all will have to do with some element of a program's design (*if* it is to be an appropriate program evaluation question). Here is a set of *generic examples of an initial set of* program evaluation questions that need to be made SMART for a *particular* program evaluation question. As you will readily note, each such generic question relates to the range of program design elements.

- To what extent have the *needs* of the *target population* been addressed through the program?

- To what degree have program *goals* been *attained*?

- To what extent can resulting program *outcomes* be *attributed* to the program?

- Have the *goals* of the program been *addressed* via the program?

- Are the program's *eligibility standards* and *criteria* being used appropriately?

- Have the program's *policies* and *procedures* been adhered to by program participants and personnel?

- How have the *methods* and *techniques* that are part of the program been applied to program personnel?

- How have the *materials, equipment,* and *facilities* associated with the program been utilized?

- To what extent have the program's *components, phases,* and *activities* been implemented as designed?

- How has the program's *budget* supported program operations?

- How have program *personnel* been utilized in support of program operations?

- To what extent are *incentives* effective with participants and/or personnel?

- Other questions

4.43 Select the most important questions to be answered, placing them into SMART program evaluation form

By successfully completing this task, you will have involved the client and others in selecting the program evaluation questions that are most important to answer. Relatedly, you will have further refined these selected questions by making each one a SMART program evaluation question.

Although a program evaluation may focus on any number of questions, professional practice and related experiences in evaluation of human services programs indicates that the range of questions that may be reasonably answered usually is from three to seven questions. However this number may exceed such a range, in particular instances. Again, a program evaluation question is one that allows for effective and efficient program planning and evaluation to occur. The matter of what are the most important questions to answer always should be referenced to particular program planning and evaluation actions and why each is necessary. Decisions about the most important program evaluation questions to be selected typically stem from focused discussion between and among yourself, the client, and other relevant stakeholders.

Once the most important program evaluation questions have been selected and agreed to by the client and others, each one of those questions can be made into SMART program evaluation questions. In this regard, professional practice and experiences associated with human services program planning and evaluation indicates that the more SMART the evaluation question, the greater the likelihood that the data will be gathered in response to the question and that people will use the resulting evaluation information for taking effective and efficient program planning and evaluation actions such as those discussed earlier in this section of this Resource Guide.

A SMART human services program evaluation question, therefore, is a question that meets the following criteria:

- **S**pecific   the question specifies exactly what is to be addressed with reference to particular aspects of the program's design (the question is not a *general* restatement of one of the above generic and example program evaluation questions).

- **M**easurable   there is a way that data can be collected on particular variables to answer the question (to be discussed under the next activity).

- **A**nswerable   there are methods, procedures, and instrumentation that can be developed and/or selected to gather data on particular variables to answer the question.

- **R**elevant   an answer to the question has been determined to be important in that the answer (evaluation information) will facilitate a program planning and evaluation action.

- **T**imeframed   the question can be answered over a prescribed period of time; and a time period before the program (baseline condition) may be necessary to adequately answer the question.

4.5 For Each Program Evaluation Question, Specify the Data Collection Variables

Through this program planning and evaluation activity, the *variables* on which data need to be collected in order to answer each program evaluation question are specified. In this regard, a *data collection variable* refers to some construct, item, event, or other matter that needs to be measured via some data collection procedure. Further, if data are collected on the variable, then those data will contribute to answering the program evaluation question; if data are not so collected, then it is less likely that a meaningful answer to the program evaluation question will be generated. For instance, for the program evaluation question, "To what *extent* have *emotionally disturbed adolescents* become more *capable of learning* in *regular classroom settings*," there are several data collection variables that can be initially identified. These are:

- Emotionally disturbed adolescents (who are these people)
- Capable of learning (how is learning capability recognized)
- Learning (what changes in what areas will indicate knowledge and/or skill acquisition)
- Regular classroom settings (what are these locations)
- Extent (how much is expected; what has occurred)

Specification of data collection variables, such as the ones listed above, involves yourself with the client and others in the following tasks *for each program evaluation question*:

4.51   List the variables on which data can be collected
4.52   Operationalize the variables on which data are to be collected

Each of these tasks will be discussed below. When you have specified these variables, they can be described/operationalized on the respective Program Evaluation Protocol Worksheet (see Figure 6.1).

4.51 List the variables on which data can be collected

To successfully accomplish this task, you first take each program evaluation question as a separate entity. Then, for each program evaluation question, the variables reflected by that question are listed. In this regard, and using the example program evaluation question noted above, relevant data collection variables are the following:

- Emotionally disturbed adolescents
- Capable of learning
- Learning
- Regular classroom setting
- Extent

4.52 Operationalize the variables on which data are to be collected

Once the variables on which data are to be collected have been identified, those variables can be operationalized for data collection purposes. By creating appropriate operational definitions for the variables, it will become clear about what kinds of data need to be collected. Relatedly, such operationalization will help guide decisions about methods, procedures, and instruments for data collection (discussed in next section).

For instance, using again the program evaluation question, "To what extent have emotionally disturbed adolescents become more capable of learning in regular classroom settings," the variables that were listed above can be operationalized. Here is an *actual example* of the operational definition of these variables:

- **Emotionally disturbed adolescents**—all students who have been validated into the program as "CORE program participants," in that they are formally classified as ED and spend more than 50% of their instructional time in the program.

- **Capable of learning**—judgments and opinions of regular classroom teachers who have instructed the participants in language arts, physical science, and history as to their capacity to attend to instruction and follow through on activities.

- **Learning**—amount and level of progress of the program participants in language arts, physical science, and history based on teacher ratings (qualitative) and report card grades (quantitative).

- **Regular classroom setting**—language arts classes, physical science classes, and history seminars that occur in the "main" high school building.

- **Extent**—the amount of progress made by the student over time, while in the program.

Once the variables have been operationalized for each program evaluation question, they can be placed on a Program Evaluation Protocol Worksheet for that question (see Figure 6.1).

4.6 Describe the Data Collection Methods, Instruments, and Procedures

Through this program planning and evaluation activity, you establish how data will be collected on the variables in order to answer each program evaluation question. In this regard, unless each evaluation question is answered in ways that are agreed to by the client and that is meaningful to them, it is unlikely that the client will be able to use the resulting information for program planning actions. Hence data collection that is targeted to particular variables and that will result in an answer to a particular program evaluation question is crucial to a sound program evaluation. Clearly, preparing for data collection and following through on it, is a "customized professional challenge."

There are several tasks that, if successfully completed, will allow data to be collected on variables that will answer a particular program evaluation question. These tasks, which need to be accomplished for each program evaluation question, are as follows:

4.61   Review the data collection variables for the most important ones.
4.62   For each variable, decide about the methods and sources for data collection.
4.63   For each variable, decide about procedures for data collection.
4.64   Develop and/or select data collection instrumentation.

Each of these tasks will be discussed below. When you have described data collection methods, instruments, and procedures for each program evaluation question, they can be placed on the respective Program Evaluation Protocol Worksheet (see Figure 6.1).

4.61 Review the data collection variables for the most important ones

To successfully complete this task, you need to consider each program evaluation question as a separate entity. Then, in relation to that question, you review all of the variables that already have been listed (see Task 4.51) and that have been operationalized (see Task 4.52). In essence, you now can decide whether all of the variables are really important enough that data should be collected on them. It is possible that, upon review and discussion with the client, there may be particular variables on which data cannot be collected due to factors such as a lack of an appropriate database, time, ethical concerns or simply that collecting data on them would not seem to help answer the program evaluation question.

Also, at this point, it is useful to decide whether there are other data collection variables that now seem important that need to be added to the list, operationalized, and placed on a Program Evaluation Protocol Worksheet (see Figure 6.1).

4.62 For each variable, decide about the methods and sources for data collection

Once the most important data collection variables have been decided upon, and operationalized, for each program evaluation question, attention now can turn to how data can be collected on the variables. In this regard, two separate, yet interrelated matters need to be decided. These decisions have to do with the following matters:

1. **Methods** for data collection.
2. **Sources** for data collection.

Methods

A *method* for data collection refers to the particular way or technology that will be used by "program evaluation personnel" to collect data on one or more variables in order to answer a program evaluation question (the notion of program evaluation personnel will be discussed in a subsequent part of this section.) Toward this end, there are a range of possible data collection methods. Naturally, the particular method used will depend on the nature of the variables and the particular program evaluation question. As such, here is a listing of generic data collection methods, recognizing full well that each method possesses advantages and limitations (in light of the data collection variables and in relation to the particular evaluation question):

- **Questionnaire**—The questionnaire method reflects use of a set of specific questions (not to be confused with program evaluation questions) that are listed as items on a survey instrument. An item (question) might be close ended (e.g. item with a 5 pt. response scale) or an open ended one. Typically, the questionnaire method for program evaluation purposes involves completion by each respondent (data source) prior to a program and at least one point in time following the program.

- **Test**—The test method reflects use of a written test, reflected in the form of test items, designed to "test" out what a respondent (e.g. program participant) knows about some topic or subject matter content. A test may be such that it is categorized in one of the following ways:

  o Norm referenced test (NRT)
  o Criterion referenced test (CRT)
  o Instructor made test (IMT)

Often, a test is given to program participants prior to and following the program as a basis for deciding whether respondents have learned/gained knowledge.

- **Permanent Product Review**—This permanent product review method reflects the use of files, official records, and databases for collecting data prior to, during, and following a program.

- **Rating Scale/Checklist**—This method reflects use of a series of behaviors or other kinds of items (e.g. "qualities of an entity") that are rated or checked off by a respondent, often at points in time prior to, during, and following a program.

- **Interview**—This method involves discussing with a person (individual interview) selected items or issues that relate to a data collection variable. In this regard, an interview may involve use of a set of prescribed items (often referred to as a "structured interview"); or a few items that are attempts to elicit a range of response (often called "informal or unstructured interview").

- **Naturalistic observation**—This method reflects direct observation of one or more respondents in naturalistic settings (e.g. classroom, office), often accompanied by use of a behavioral rating sheet, checklist, or other systematic behavioral assessment scheme.

Sources

A *data source* refers to a particular individual, group, or other entity (e.g. program records) on which data will be generated for program evaluation purposes. Typically, a data source is referred to as a respondent or respondent group. As such, there are a variety of respondents which may be data sources depending, of course, on the nature of the data collection variables and particular program evaluation question. These types of data sources include the following:

- **Target Population**—usually a data source when data are to be collected on variables having to do with learning, perceptions, related reactions, or improvements in functioning or performance of the target population.

- **Program Personnel**—who are requested to make ratings, judgments, or provide other kinds of data on program participants.

- **Files, Records, Databases**—that contain relevant data related to particular variables.

- **Other People**—whose reactions or judgments about the human services program are important and that also are related to particular variables.

4.63 For each variable, decide about procedures for data collection

To successfully accomplish this task, it is necessary to decide how you and others need to *proceed* in order to collect the data on the specified variables in order to answer the particular program evaluation question. In this sense, "how to proceed" reflects when data are to be collected relative to the time that the program is/will be implemented and also whether the program will serve as its own control (N=1 Situation) or whether other controls will be used (Comparison Group Situation).

N=1 Situation

This reflects a situation where the program is its own control. In this regard, the program is best considered as a case, an "n" of "1", with no comparison group. As such, there are three main types of data collection procedures that may be used in this kind of situation. These are:

- **Preprogram/Post program procedure**—where data are collected prior to the program and at the conclusion of the program (two points in time).

- **Time series procedure**—where data are collected prior to, during, at the conclusion of, and following the program at prespecified/numerous points in time.

- **Post program procedure**—data are collected only at the conclusion of the program.

Naturally, there are advantages, limitations, and reasons having to do with use of the above kinds of procedures, discussed in depth in publications by Herson and Barlow; Nelson; and Kratochwill (which can be found in the References section at the end of this book).

Comparison Group Situation

This reflects a situation where the program is compared to an alternative/appropriate program or to a "no-program" condition. As such, there are also three types of data collection procedures that may be used in a comparison group situation. These are:

- **Preprogram/post program procedure**—data are collected on the target groups of both programs prior to and at the conclusion of the program (two points in time).

- **Time series procedure**—data are collected relative to the target groups of both programs at prescribed/numerous points prior to, during, at the conclusion of, and following the program.

- **Post program procedure**—data are collected only at the conclusion of the program relative to both programs.

Here, too, there are advantages, limitations, and reasons for use of each procedure, discussed in depth in publications by Cook and Campbell; Campbell and Stanley which are found in the References and Resources section at the end of this book).

4.64 Develop and/or select data collection instrumentation

Once data collection methods, sources of data, and procedures have been determined (or concomitant with these decisions), the task to be successfully accomplished has to do with data collection instruments. In this regard, a particular instrument may already exist that can be defended as appropriate for use in data collection. In this case, the more specific task has to do with *instrument selection*. On other occasions, perhaps most of them, the specific task has to do with *instrument development*.

In making instrument selection and/or development decisions with respect to human services program evaluation, there are four "qualities of an instrument" that need to be considered by the client and other relevant stakeholders in concert with yourself. These qualities are:

- **Practical**—the instrument can be used as part of the program evaluation in ways that do not disrupt operational routines of the program and organization.

- **Useful**—the instrument will allow data to be collected in order to answer a particular evaluation question.

- **Proper**—the instrument can be used in ways that adhere to all relevant legal requirements and ethical standards.

- **Technically Defensible**—the instrument can be defended/justified in terms of its reliability and validity, given a particular program evaluation question.

4.7 Describe the Methods and Procedures for Data Analysis

Through this program planning and evaluation activity, you determine how the data that have been collected will be analyzed in order to answer each program evaluation question. In this regard, data that have been collected serve as the basis for analyzing and interpreting those results so that it can be communicated to the client and other relevant stakeholders as evaluation information. As such, it is the communicated evaluation information that is considered as a response (answer) to each particular program evaluation question. Unless the data that have been collected are analyzed in a systematic way and interpreted with respect to an appropriate frame of reference, it is not likely that a program evaluation question will be answered in a manner that informs yourself, the client, and other key stakeholders. Consequently, these people will not be informed about how to take program planning actions. Thus, the extent to which program planning and evaluation can contribute to adding value will be limited.

There are several tasks that, if successfully accomplished, will allow data to be analyzed and interpreted using practical, technically sound methods and procedures. These tasks, which need to be accomplished with respect to each program evaluation question, are as follow:

4.71   Select the units of analysis
4.72   Organize and display data
4.73   Identify the frames of reference
4.74   Determine statistical procedures

Each of these tasks will be discussed below. When you have accomplished them for each program evaluation question, place the information on the respective Program Evaluation Protocol Worksheet (see Figure 6.1).

4.71 Select the units of analysis

To successfully complete the task, you make a determination about how the data are to be divided into units. In this regard, a unit is a particular segment, group, or division in which data that have been collected can be placed. Although the particular units of analysis are dependent on the program evaluation question and data collection variables, *examples* of generic units typically used as part of human service program evaluation are the following:

- An individual (student, worker, organization, etc.)
- A group of individual units (people, departments)
- A set of group units (all classrooms in a school)
- Other units

Naturally, the exact units need to be clearly conceptualized and operationalized as part of each protocol.

4.72 *Organize and display the data*

To successfully accomplish this task, a decision is made by yourself and the client (along with a program planning and evaluation team if one exists) about how to place the data *in order* and how to display the data. This task, naturally, occurs relative to the units of analysis relative to each program evaluation question.

There are many ways, of course, in which data can be organized and displayed as part of data analysis. In particular, here are some *examples*:

1. Flow Chart
Purpose: To visually diagram or chart the process followed by a program, product, or service that enables people to: (a) understand the process; and (b) record and display data having to do with the process.

2. Histogram
Purpose: To display the frequency of distribution of data so that people can make judgments about the centrality and variability of the distribution.

3. Checksheet
Purpose: To gather data based on a series of observations so that people can determine the frequency of a problem or event.

4. Cause and Effect Diagram
Purpose: To identify possible causes of a pinpointed problem, need, or area of concern so that people can determine most important "causes" relative to data associated with the "causes".

5. Pareto Chart
Purpose: To determine the relative importance of all the problems or conditions so that people can identify the most basic "cause".

6. Time Series Chart
Purpose: To display data in a series of data points, over a period of time, to examine changes and trends in the data.

7. Scatter Diagram

Purpose: To display in graphic form the relationship between two corresponding variables along a horizontal axis and vertical axis.

8. Control Chart

Purpose: To display in graphic form the extent to which a process, such as a program implementation process, is in or out of expected control.

4.73 Identify the frames of reference

To successfully accomplish this task, the frames of reference to which data will be considered as part of the analysis are identified. In this regard, a frame of reference is some point, level of response, time period, or other entity such as a database (normative) to which program evaluation data that have been collected will be compared. Once this comparison is made, it then is possible to interpret the data in terms of its meaning. There are, of course, many specific reference frames that can be used for data analysis and interpretation. Generic reference frames, however, that may be appropriate for use with a particular program evaluation question, and its data collection variable, are the following:

- **Normative Reference Frame**—where data are compared to a statistical norm or norm group.

- **Criterion Reference Frame**—where data are compared to a specific, previously established criterion level.

- **Point in Time Reference Frame**—where data collected at one point in time (e.g. preprogram) are compared to data collected at another point in time (post program). This frame of reference is likely to be used in conjunction with one of the above two reference frames.

4.74 Determine statistical procedures

To successfully accomplish this task, a decision needs to be made about particular statistical procedures to be used as part of the analysis. To make this kind of determination, however, various matters must be considered that are listed below. These include:

- The nature of the data (nominal, ordinal, interval, ratio).

- The amount of data, given the units of analysis ("n").

- Whether there are appropriate comparison groups or whether the program is an "n of 1".

- The program evaluation question.

- The informational needs and technical understanding of the people who will use the resulting evaluation information for program planning actions.

- Other considerations, specific to the program being evaluated and its relevant context.

Additional information about the determination of statistical procedures can be found in the References and Resources section at the end of this book.

4.8 Specify Program Evaluation Personnel and Responsibilities

Through this program planning and evaluation activity, the people who will be involved in the program evaluation, in some capacity other than as data sources, are identified. Then, their roles as evaluation personnel are clarified, and their responsibilities as part of the evaluation are determined. With clear specification of evaluation personnel and their responsibilities, the likelihood is increased that each program evaluation protocol will be carried out as expected. Without successful completion of this program evaluation activity, however, the chances of program evaluation protocol utilization is greatly reduced. This is so because what is to occur as part of the evaluation, by whom, and when will be ambiguous.

There are several tasks that, if successfully accomplished, will allow the evaluation to proceed according to the program evaluation protocols. These tasks, which need to be accomplished with respect to each program evaluation question, are as follows:

4.81 Identify the evaluation responsibilities that need to be fulfilled and when (timelines).
4.82 Determine the people who will be responsible.
4.83 Discuss the timelines and responsibilities with the people.

Each of the above tasks will be considered below. When you have accomplished these tasks for each program evaluation question, place the information on the respective Program Evaluation Protocol Worksheet (Figure 6.1).

4.81 Identify the evaluation responsibilities that need to be fulfilled and when (timelines)

To successfully accomplish this program planning and evaluation task, you identify the *specific evaluation* responsibilities that need to be fulfilled so that *each* program evaluation question can be answered in a sound way. Relatedly, the *timeframes* within which the evaluation responsibilities must be carried out also need to be delineated by yourself in conjunction with the client and the program planning and evaluation team (if one is being used). Naturally, this task is to occur for each program evaluation question.

With respect to specific evaluation responsibilities, they can be readily determined by reviewing a copy of the respective Program Evaluation Protocol Worksheet (see Figure 6.1) under the section for data collection methods, procedures, and instruments and under the section for methods and procedures for data analysis.

Upon review of that information, a range of evaluation responsibilities are likely to be identified. Although the *specific* wording of the evaluation responsibilities will depend on the particular protocol, many of the responsibilities will be of the following kind (not an all-inclusive listing):

- Distribution of instruments
- Collection of instruments
- Conducting interviews (individual; group)
- Coding interview data and analyzing results
- Analyzing and interpreting survey data
- Data entry/computing/reporting
- Training data collectors/behavioral observers
- Other tasks (responsibilities).

With respect to evaluation timeframe, the responsibilities need to be made specific for each particular responsibility. Otherwise, the chances are increased that the evaluation protocol will not be utilized as intended by those so responsible.

4.82 Determine the people who will be responsible

To successfully accomplish this task, each specific evaluation responsibility that has been determined is reviewed by yourself and the client. Then, a decision is made as to what individuals are able to fulfill the responsibility, give the timeframe for it. Naturally, in some situations, approval, other authorization, or released professional time may need to be obtained so that a particular individual can be given the responsibility and be able to fulfill it.

The range of possibilities is numerous for the people who may be responsible for aspects of a program evaluation, as referenced to a particular program evaluation protocol. In many instances, though, the following kinds of people are likely to have responsibilities for aspects of any human services program evaluation. The kinds of people include the following categories:

- Consultants (internal, external)
- Staff (e.g., teachers, psychologists)
- Administrators (e.g., building principals; middle managers)
- Executives (e.g., assistant superintendent; president)
- Other.

4.83 Discuss the timeline and responsibilities with the people

This task can be successfully accomplished in a twofold manner for each program evaluation question. First, a Program Evaluation Control Chart (see Table 6.1) can be completed, such as the example chart shown below. Second, the responsible people can meet with you, the client, or other appropriate parties to discuss their responsibilities and the timeline.

Table 6.1: Program Evaluation Control Chart

Program: Site: Date:

Program Evaluation Question	Evaluation Responsibilities	Personnel	Timeframe	Comments

4.9 Delineate Guidelines for Communication and Use of Program Evaluation Information

Through this program planning and evaluation activity, guidelines are provided for the client and other key stakeholders in how to communicate the resulting evaluation information as well as how to use such information for program planning. In this respect, communication and use of program evaluation information by all relevant parties affected by the human services program is a major activity of the overall program planning and evaluation process. Without successful completion of this activity, therefore, the entire program evaluation endeavor can be questioned by all individuals involved with the process. With successful completion of this activity, however, the likelihood is increased that program planning actions will be charted and instituted, contributing to continuous program development and improvement.

With respect to this program planning and evaluation activity, *communication* of program evaluation information means conveying the results (i.e., answers to a particular program evaluation question) to targeted audiences, through written and oral methods, in ways that inform those audiences. Relatedly, *use* of program evaluation information refers to the involvement of people in reviewing the program evaluation information, considering its meaning, and then deciding what program planning actions are appropriate to take to develop and improve the program.

There are several tasks that, if successfully accomplished, will contribute to effective communication and use of program evaluation information. These tasks, which need to be successfully completed for each program evaluation question, are the following ones:

4.91 Target the audiences for receipt of evaluation information.

4.92 Specify what evaluation information is to be communicated, how, by whom, and when, to target audiences.

4.93 Determine how to involve target audiences in use of evaluation information.

4.94 Pinpoint program planning actions.

Each of the above tasks will be considered below. When you have accomplished them for each program evaluation question, place the information on the respective Program Evaluation Protocol Worksheet (Figure 6.1).

4.91 Target the audiences for receipt of evaluation information

To successfully accomplish this task, you identify the individuals and groups to whom feedback or receipt of program evaluation information is warranted. In essence, these target audiences are people who are affected by the program in some way (i.e., "have a stake" in it) and who may be able to contribute to program development and improvement with use of meaningful, timely evaluation information. In this regard, there are a range of individuals and groups who are candidates for being target audiences for program evaluation information. These audiences include the following:

- Administrators who oversee the program
- Program implementers
- Program supervisors
- Funders of the program
- Program participants
- Policymakers in various state and federal agencies
- Other individuals and groups who have an appropriate stake in the program.

Once these possible target audiences are identified, it is recommended that the contributions to the program and its continuous development, through receipt of evaluation information, be made explicit. Through such explication, it will become clearer as to who are the priority target audiences. In this regard, examples of contributions that may be made by means of receipt of program evaluation information by target audiences are:

- Assistance in revision of one or more program elements
- Help in marketing the program
- Authorization of continued funds
- Public endorsement of the program
- Other contributions.

4.92 Specify what evaluation information is to be communicated, how, by whom, and when, to target audiences

Once the target audiences for receipt of evaluation information have been identified, decisions need to be made by yourself, the client, and other relevant stakeholders about what is to be communicated, along with several interrelated matters. Toward this end, the

Program Evaluation Information Chart (see Table 6.2) has proven to be a useful tool. In that regard, the following definitions apply:

- Target Audiences (as previously identified above)
- Nature of Information (e.g., graphs, tables, lists, narrative relative to a program evaluation question)
- How to Communicate (e.g., written report; meeting; videotape)
- Communicator (e.g., consultant, program director)
- Timeframe for Communication (e.g., specific day; week).

Table 6.2: Program Evaluation Information Chart

Program: Site: Date:

Target Audience	Nature of Information	How to Communicate	Communicator	Timeframe for Communication

4.93 Determine how to involve target audiences in use of evaluation information

For target audiences to be involved in use of program evaluation information as a basis for contributing to continuous development and improvement of the human services program, these people need to experience a meaningful process. Toward this end, the Program Evaluation Planning Forum has been determined to be a meaningful experiential, involvement approach.

Program Evaluation/Planning Forum

The procedures described below are for application by a committee of target audience members, in order to assist members with successful completion of the task of utilization of program evaluation information.

117

1. Each program evaluation protocol contained in a Program Evaluation Plan typically contains at least one program evaluation instrument. Each such instrument is used to collect data that will help answer the particular program evaluation question. In this regard, each instrument is numbered in a way that corresponds to the number of the program evaluation protocol and question to which it relates. For example, Instrument 3 would be the instrument used to collect data to help answer Program Evaluation Question 3, which is part of Program Evaluation Protocol 3. Relatedly, each instrument is structured in terms of a range of instrument items. For most instruments, these items reflect specific questions or statements to which each respondent provided a numerical rating, typically on a two point, three point, four point, or five point scale, depending on the nature of the item.

2. When all data collection instruments are completed, these data are printed on tables. Each table has a number that corresponds to a particular data collection instrument. The items on the table reflect the same items as the instrument. A completed table includes descriptive statistical summary results (e.g., percentages, means, modes) for each of the items. For instance, Table 3 would display summary results derived from Instrument 3 that relates to Program Evaluation Question 3, that is part of Program Evaluation Protocol 3.

3. When the data have been collected and processed for each program evaluation question, the tables that display those data are provided to the members of the committee responsible for the question. Once the tables have been received by the committee, they schedule a Program Evaluation/Planning Forum that reflects a projected 45 minute to 1 hour timeframe.

4. In preparation for the Forum, each member of the committee is asked to review the tables and any other relevant evaluation information pertinent to the question. Such review is to occur independently, by each committee member, in order to familiarize him/herself with the results and to generate ideas about their meaning and about implications for planning program improvement actions.

5. At the Forum, the committee focuses their attention and discussion on a set of separate, yet interrelated questions for each and every table. The discussion questions, for each table, are:

   5.1 For each item in the table, what do the data indicate:
      5.11 An expected (satisfactory) result?
      5.12 A more than expected result?
      5.13 A less than expected result?
      5.14 An ambiguous result that requires additional data to provide a clearer meaning?

   5.2 For the table overall, what can be said, confidently, about the results?

5.21 What kinds of evaluative judgments can be made about what particular program design elements?

5.211 Need for change?

5.212 Continuation?

5.213 Expansion/replication in other areas?

5.214 Termination/phasing out?

The committee documents their discussion in writing, especially consensus about answers to the above discussion questions.

6. The discussion activities delineated in procedure 5 above occur for each table for each program evaluation question. Then, once all tables have been discussed for the question, the committee composes a program evaluation summary statement. In essence, the summary statement is the committee's answer to the particular program evaluation question. It can be submitted to yourself or the client.

4.94 Pinpoint program planning actions

This task can be successfully accomplished, if it is part of the Program Evaluation/ Planning Forum. Thus, the same committee(s) focuses on actions that are indicated that can contribute to continuing improvement of some aspect of the human resources program. Using the evaluation results displayed in the tables and the program evaluation summary statement, the committee discusses and answers the following set of separate yet interrelated questions:

1. What kinds of program improvement actions are indicated, based on the program evaluation information that we (committee) have considered for this particular program evaluation question:

1.1 Revisions in eligibility criteria for participants?

1.2 Alterations in the nature, scope, or substance of educational goals and objectives?

1.3 Content changes?

1.4 Revisions in instructional methods and materials?

1.5 Changes in experiences, settings, and/or facilities?

1.6 Resequencing or retiming of participant learning activities?

1.7 Revisions in program policies and operational procedures?

1.8 Changes in roles, responsibilities, and relationships between and among personnel and participants?

1.9 Budget requests or alterations?

1.10 Other relevant program improvement actions?

2. For *each* and *every* program improvement action that has been discussed, specified, and documented by the committee with respect to the above questions, the committee then considers and documents answers to the following:

2.1 Who needs to be involved to assure that the specific action is authorized, sanctioned, implemented, and accomplished?

119

2.2   For this specific action, what is the item frame within which authorization, sanction, implementation, and accomplishment are to occur?

2.3   For this specific action, what will be the observable and measurable evidence that it has been authorized, sanctioned, implemented, and accomplished?

2.4   As a final "security check", why are we (committee) recommending this action. Will it really contribute to enhancement of the quality and effectiveness of the program?

3.   Answers to all of the program improvement action discussion questions described by procedure 2 and 3 above can be recorded on a Program Evaluation Action Chart (see Table 6.3). This chart can then be used by the client for use in monitoring follow through on the actions.

Table 6.3: Program Evaluation Action Chart

Program: Site: Date:

Improvement Action	People to be involved	Timeframe	Accomplishment	Rational for action

4.10 Construct Program Evaluation Protocols

Through this program planning and evaluation activity, program evaluation protocols are constructed and placed in written form as a program evaluation plan document. This activity is readily accomplished if you have been completing a Program Evaluation Protocol Worksheet (Figure 6.1) for each program evaluation question, and if you have successfully completed the nine previous activities above of the Evaluation Phase.

At this point in the program planning and evaluation process, you and the client no doubt are very familiar with the notion of the program evaluation protocol. However, in order to reinforce this familiarity, the elements of a program evaluation protocol are presented again as follows:

- The program evaluation question
- Data collection variables
- Data collection methods, instruments, procedures
- Methods and procedures for data analysis
- Guidelines for communication and use of evaluation information.

When program evaluation protocols are constructed and placed in written form, they can be merged into a program evaluation plan document. In essence, the program evaluation plan is the document that is referenced for such things as when there are questions or concerns about the nature and scope of the program evaluation, how the program evaluation relates to program planning, or other matters pertaining to implementation of the program evaluation. Although there are many formats for a written program evaluation plan document, here is a particular format that has proved useful:

Program Evaluation Plan Format
I.   Overview of the Program Evaluation
    A.   Client and Client Information Needs
    B.   Timeframe of the Evaluation
II. Description of the Program that was Evaluated
III. List of Program Evaluation Questions
IV. Program Evaluation Protocols
    (one protocol for each program evaluation question, using the headings of the Program Evaluation Protocol Worksheet)
Appendix A: Copies of instruments, referenced to program evaluation protocols and questions (these may also be included as part of each protocol)
Appendix B: (optional, but desirable for external consultants) Professional biographical sketch of consultant/program planning and evaluation team

4.11 Implement the Program Evaluation

Through this program planning and evaluation activity, the program evaluation actually is implemented, based on the descriptions of the methods, procedures, and instruments contained on the program evaluation protocols. In essence, the concern at this point is to make sure that the *process* of the program evaluation is controlled in a way that is expected, based on the following *expected* process control indicators for *each* program evaluation question (protocol):

- Data are collected on the variables specified in the protocol

- Data are collected on the variables, using the methods, instruments, and procedures contained in the protocol

- Data are analyzed and interpreted, based on the methods and procedures described in the protocol

- The evaluation information that results as an answer to the question is communicated to target evaluation audiences and used by them for program planning, based on procedures delineated in the protocol.

Naturally, as the program evaluation proceeds, it may be necessary to adjust the process and revise one or more protocols. When these situations occur, the rationale for changes is to be made clear, with appropriate justifications appended to the particular program evaluation protocol.

4.12 Evaluate the Program Evaluation

Through this program planning and evaluation activity, the program evaluation that has been implemented is evaluated itself. Such "evaluation of the evaluation" occurs so that you, the client, and other relevant stakeholders can decide how future program evaluations can be improved so that they can better serve program planning actions as well as the entire program planning and evaluation process.

An evaluation of the program evaluation need not be a cumbersome, time consuming event. Rather, it can be facilitated by using the four qualities of a sound human services program, initially identified and discussed earlier in this chapter. Toward this end, four "meta-evaluation questions can be raised, with responses to the questions being obtained from the range of people who have been involved in the evaluation as personnel, data sources, client, and target evaluation audiences. These four questions are:

Practicality
1. To what extent was the program evaluation conducted in a way that allowed for its successful accomplishment?

Utility
2. In what ways was the resulting program evaluation information helpful to people? Which people?

Propriety
3. Did the program evaluation occur in a way that adhered to legal strictures and ethical standards?

Technical Defensibility
4. To what degree can the evaluation be justified with respect to matters of reliability and validity?

Response to these four questions can be obtained by means of individual interview, group discussions, and/or survey instrumentation.

references and resources

The references in this section of the book are intended to supplement coverage of the material found in the prior chapters of this book. In this respect, they serve as additional resources for learning about aspects of the planning and evaluating of human services programs. Most students who have taken the program planning and evaluation course which I taught have found these references to be helpful to them.

American Educational Research Association, American Psychological Association, and National Council on Measurement in Education. 1999. *Standards for Educational and Psychological Testing.* Washington, DC: American Psychological Association.

Barlow, D.H., and M. Hersen. 1976. *Single Case Experimental Designs.* New York: Pergamon.

Campbell, D.T., and J.C Stanley. 1966. *Experimental and Quasi- Experimental Designs for Research.* Chicago: Rand McNally.

Cook, T.D., and D.T. Campbell. 1979. *Quasi-Experimental Designs for Field Research.* Chicago: Rand McNally.

Gilbert. T. 1978. *Human Competence: Engineering Worthy Performance.* New York: McGraw Hill.

Issac, S.J., and W.B. Michael. 1997. *Handbook of Research and Evaluation,* Third Edition. San Diego: Educational and Industrial Testing Services.

Joint Committee on Standards for Educational Evaluation. 1988. *The Personnel Evaluation Standards.* Thousand Oaks, CA: Sage.

Joint Committee on Standards for Educational Evaluation. 1994. *The Program Evaluation Standards; How to Assess Evaluations of Educational Programs.* Thousand Oaks, CA: Sage.

Kaufman, R. 2000. *Mega Planning: Practical Tools for Organizational Success.* Thousand Oaks, CA: Sage.

Kiresuk, T.J., A. Smith, and J.E. Cardillo. 1994. *Goal Attainment Scaling: Applications, Theory, and Measurement.* Hillsdale, NJ: Lawrence Erlbaum.

Kratochwill, T.R., and J.R. Levin, eds. 1992. *Single-Case Research Design and Analysis.* Hillsdale, NJ: Lawrence Erlbaum.

Lincoln, Y.S. and E.G. Guba. 1985. *Naturalistic Inquiry.* Newbury Park, CA: Sage.

Love, A. 1991. *Internal Evaluation: Building Organizations from Within.* Thousand Oaks, CA: Sage.

Maher, C.A., and R.E. Bennett. 1984. *Planning and Evaluating Special Education Services.* Englewood Cliffs, NJ: Prentice Hall.

Mertens, D.M. 2005. *Research and Evaluation in Education and Psychology,* Second Edition. Thousand Oaks, CA: Sage.

Miller, G.A. 1978. *Living Systems.* New York: Macmillan.

Miller, G.A., E. Galanter, and K.H. Pribram. 1960. *Plans and the Structure of Human Behavior.* New York: Macmillan.

Patton, M.Q. 2002. *Qualitative Evaluation and Research Methods.* Newbury Park, CA: Sage.

Stake, R.E. 1995. *The Art of Case Study Research.* Thousand Oaks, CA: Sage.

Stufflebeam, D.L., G.F. Madaus, and T. Kellaghan. 2000. *Evaluation Models: Viewpoints on Educational and Human Services Evaluation.* Boston: Kluwer.

Von Bertalanffy, L. 1968. *General Systems Theory.* London: Penguin.

Watzlawick, P., J. Weakland, and R. Fisch. 1984. *Change: Principles of Problem Formation and Problem Resolution.* New York: Norton.

Yin, R. 1994. *Case Study Research: Design and Methods.* Newbury Park, CA: Sage.

about the author

Dr. Charles A. Maher has over 35 years of experience, worldwide in teaching, research, and practice about the planning and evaluation of human services programs and systems. His work and contributions in human services span many and diverse areas: special education and general education programs in public schools and related educational agencies; mental health centers and social services delivery systems; corporate training and leadership development entities; military units; and sport and performance psychology at professional and collegiate levels.. Dr. Maher is Professor Emeritus of Psychology, Graduate School of Applied and Professional Psychology, Rutgers University. He has served as Chair of the Department of Applied Psychology and as Director of the School Psychology Doctoral Program of this graduate school unit. Currently, he is actively involved as a sport and performance psychologist and he is Director of Psychological Services for the Cleveland Indians Baseball Organization. Before embarking on his academic career, Dr. Maher was a public school administrator, school psychologist, a teacher of students with disabilities, and a basketball and baseball coach in high school and college. Dr. Maher is a licensed psychologist and a fellow of several psychological societies. He has authored and edited a range of books and has published many articles in the above areas in refereed journals. Dr. Maher continues to be actively engaged in the professional practice of psychology in areas of education, business, sport, and performance.